GRESLEY'S

A4s
THE BR ERA
IN COLOUR

An illustrated survey of the thirty-four A4 Class Pacifics
which plied the East Coast Main Line during
the formative years of British Railways.

Compiled with illustrations from the
Keith Pirt Collection

BOOK LAW PUBLICATIONS

Copyright Book Law Publications
ISBN 978-1-907094-24-8

INTRODUCTION

This album has been compiled from the colour transparencies created by Keith Pirt during his most prolific period photographing the motive power of British Railways. The Gresley A4s were perhaps his favourite class of steam locomotive and Keith's visits to the East Coast Main Line, especially around Retford, gave him ample opportunity to capture the magnificent Pacifics in all their guises on the stretch of BR where they performed their most important work. He managed to 'bag' each and every one of the class at some point in their lives, be they on shed, works, heading the premier expresses between London and Edinburgh, or hauling some mundane goods working. Besides the aforementioned junction, KRP had lineside permits to walk virtually the length of the former Great Northern section of the ECML, so the locations are many and varied. During the latter years of the class, when the surviving members were working on the so called '3-hour expresses' between Aberdeen and Glasgow, visits were made to the north-east of Scotland too.

The locomotives are illustrated in the order in which they were built at Doncaster. So, what might at first appear to be a haphazard presentation has in fact been carefully put together to provide the reader with a sense of chronology of how the class slowly evolved. Naturally the period in review was the time when all of the class wore the standard Brunswick green livery of BR so to counter what might be regarded as a 'sameness' we have provided a table for each locomotive which lists the important milestones in the history of that locomotive; included in the table is a summary of the various liveries carried by each over the decades when they were operational.

Finally, the Publisher would like to thank Gavin Morrison for the use of certain images which filled some rather apparent gaps during the preparation of this volume. Thanks Gavin.

Cover illustration: See page 48.
Rear cover, top: See page 56.
Rear cover, bottom: See page 37.

First published in the United Kingdom by
BOOK LAW PUBLICATIONS 2013
382 Carlton Hill, Nottingham, NG4 1JA
Printed and bound by The Amadeus Press, Cleckheaton, West Yorkshire.

GRESLEY'S A4s: THE BR ERA - IN COLOUR

CONTENTS

60014

Built: Doncaster, No.1818.

Put into traffic: 7th September 1935.

Original number: 2509.

Subsequent numbers:
    14 14th June 1946.
60014 22nd June 1949.

Name: SILVER LINK.

Livery details:
Silver Grey unlined: 7th September 1935 to 20th October 1937.
Garter Blue with red and white lining: 6th December 1937 to 20th October 1941.
Black unlined: 6th December 1941 to 22nd May 1946.
Garter Blue with red and white lining: 14th June 1946 to 9th May 1949.
Dark Blue with black and white lining: 22nd June 1949 to 3rd December 1951.
Brunswick Green with orange and black lining: 4th January 1952 to breaking up.

Side skirting removed: 6th December 1941.

Double chimney fitted: 30th October 1957.

Last major overhaul completed: 12th April 1961 General - Doncaster.

Last shed: King's Cross since 31st May 1950.

Condemned: 29th December 1962.

Subsequent fate: Entered Doncaster Works for cutting-up 16th January 1963.

Comment: *Considering the prestige of the class and being the pioneer engine, No.60014 should have been an immediate candidate for preservation. Alas, official vandalism won the day and being due for a major overhaul, the locomotive was instead written off and broken up shortly after entering 'The Plant'.*

(above) The senior member of the A4 Class, No.60014 SILVER LINK descends Gamston bank with a Down express in late August 1961. The front end of the Pacific looks nothing short of immaculate, even in the shadow of the late afternoon sun. Methinks the splendid external condition possibly stems from the A4 being involved with a special working; note the coupling hook which has also had some special treatment. There are thirteen vehicles behind the tender; quite a normal load for these ECML express trains at that period but there is nothing special about this train.

(opposite, top) Earlier in that same month of the summer of 1961, No.60014 was captured on film with an Up working of *THE ELIZABETHAN* and is passing Markham Moor summit with very little exhaust to show for its efforts. The same external finish presented in the previous illustration is obvious in this one too. Perhaps regular employment hauling this prestige express saw the A4 given special treatment by the cleaners at King's Cross shed.

(opposite, bottom) Same summer, same month, same engine, same train but in this case the Down working at a different location. This is the Edinburgh bound train just outside Hatfield in August 1961 with our A4 still maintaining that museum like finish. It is a shame that no one in the BR hierarchy saw fit to preserve this particular A4 once it was withdrawn. Basically we had the wrong people holding office in the upper echelons of BR and the various Government departments dealing with such things at that time.

(above) Leaving Hadley Wood tunnel behind, No.60015 QUICKSILVER lives up to its name as it hurries north with an express in August 1961. Another of the King's Cross allocation, its bears the hallmark of the burnished buffer heads and front coupling gear. Note the nameplate has a red background on this date.

(opposite, top) Prior to being seconded for the *ELIZABETHAN* duties and receiving that dynamic clean and polish, SILVER LINK waits in the yard at Grantham shed in June 1961 for a southbound working. No stranger to this depot, No.60014 spent two periods of its life allocated to Grantham 16th August 1944 to 30th May 1948, and 16th June 1948 to 31st May 1950 whilst the rest of its existence was spent at 34A 'Top Shed'.

(opposite, bottom) With only twelve on today, No.60014 runs easily past the photographer at Ganwick corner as it heads north with another express in September 1961. The electrification warning flashes seem to have been fitted during late August 1961 as the previous pictures taken prior to that time show the engine bereft of such things. The ATC/AWS was fitted to this engine as early as September 1950 when the scheme was at an experimental stage. A small number of the A4 class were fitted in order to test the effectiveness of the equipment on the former GN main line (for the record, a small number of WD 2-8-0s working from GN line sheds were also fitted with the ATC at the same time).

60015

Built: Doncaster, No.1819.

Put into traffic: 21st September 1935.

Original number: 2510.

Subsequent numbers:
    15 12th September 1946.
60015 17th December 1948.

Name: QUICKSILVER.

Livery details:
Silver Grey unlined: 21st September 1935 to 12th April 1938.
Garter Blue with red and white lining: 28th May 1938 to 20th August 1943.
Black unlined: 5th October 1943 to 13th August 1947.
Garter Blue with red and white lining: 4th October 1947 to 18th October 1949.
Dark Blue with black and white lining: 25th November 1949 to 17th October 1951.
Brunswick Green with orange and black lining: 22nd November 1951 to breaking up.

Side skirting removed: 7th November 1941.

Double chimney fitted: 9th August 1957.

Last major overhaul completed: 13th January 1961 General - Doncaster.

Last shed: King's Cross since 9th September 1951.

Condemned: 25th April 1963.

Subsequent fate: Entered Doncaster Works for cutting-up 10th May 1963.

Comment: *First of the class (admittedly only four strong at the time) to have longer buffers fitted after a tragic accident, in July 1936, revealed there was inadequate clearance with the original buffers.*

Twelve months earlier the camera has captured No.60015 leaning around the curve at the south end of the Retford crossover as it heads for home with an Up express on a sunny afternoon in July 1960. The nameplate at this time has a black background.

March 1962 and with remnants of snow on the ground and a stiff easterly wind blowing, No.60015 leaves Gainsborough Lea Road station behind whilst working a diverted Up express. For all their positive points, the A4s had just as many negative points, one of which was the intensive maintenance required to keep them in top class condition. Although this engine emerged from its final General overhaul on 13th January 1961, it returned thereafter to Doncaster shops on no less than four occasions for Casual Light repairs during the ensuing two year period prior to withdrawal.

Making a nice bit of smoke, No.60015 climbs Gamston bank at Eaton Wood with a morning express for King's Cross in late June 1960. Note the 'reversed' train headboard attached to the middle lamp iron. This reveals one of the methods used to return a headboard back to King's Cross shed. The shape and size opens a couple of possibilities of what the headboard might indicate on the face side *YORKSHIRE PULLMAN* or *TEES-TYNE PULLMAN*. The A4 may well have worked either of those on the previous evening, one to Leeds, the other to Newcastle. We can only speculate as to which one it really was. *(below)* Another evening working for QUICKSILVER! It is now September 1962 and the location is just south of Retford where the old A1 road bridge crossed the ECML. The chime whistle has just sounded as both a warning and a greeting to Keith Pirt. ATC was fitted to this engine in February 1953 during the protracted period when it was still experimental. 1962 proved to be No.60015's last summer of work. It would pay one more visit to Doncaster for repair during November and December but by the following April it would be laid-up and then condemned at 34A; it made the final journey to Doncaster and oblivion a couple of weeks later.

60016

Built: Doncaster, No.1821.

Put into traffic: 5th November 1935.

Original number: 2511.

Subsequent numbers:
16 17th November 1946.
60016 11th June 1948.

Name: SILVER KING.

Livery details:
Silver Grey unlined: 5th November 1935 to 11th June 1938.
Garter Blue with red and white lining: 9th August 1938 to 11th March 1943.
Black unlined: 10th April 1943 to 1st April 1947.
Garter Blue with red and white lining: 10th May 1947 to 13th September 1949.
Dark Blue with black and white lining: 21st October 1949 to 4th June 1952.
Brunswick Green with orange and black lining: 10th July 1952 to breaking up.

Side skirting removed: 10th April 1943.

Double chimney fitted: 13th June 1957.

Last major overhaul completed: 17th August 1962 General - Doncaster.

Last shed: Aberdeen Ferryhill from 10th November 1963.

Condemned: 19th March 1965.

Subsequent fate: Sold for scrap to Motherwell Machinery & Scrap Co. Wishaw, May 1965.

Comment: *After being initially allocated to King's Cross shed for just thirteen days, this A4 was transferred to Gateshead and was never again allocated to a shed south of that depot. That transfer of 18th November 1935 was purely to have No.2511 as stand-by engine to work the 10 a.m. SILVER JUBILEE from Newcastle to London in case any of the three King's Cross engines failed whilst over-nighting at Gateshead. After the SJ had departed, No.2511 then worked to Edinburgh with the 11.10 a.m. express ex Leeds.*

(above) Passing Leeman Road sidings, No.60016 SILVER KING leaves York with a Newcastle express in May 1959. Up to this time, the A4 had spent the whole of its life (excepting the first two weeks shedded at King's Cross) allocated to depots on Tyneside and had been the 'spare' engine stationed at the northern end of the *SILVER JUBILEE* route in pre-war years. Shortly after the outbreak of hostilities in September 1939 it was transferred from Gateshead to Heaton from the centre of the potential target to the peripheral so to speak. Returning to Gateshead at the end of March 1943, it was again moved to Heaton five weeks later and did not go back to Gateshead until the first month of 1945. Not all of Gateshead's A4s went through this transferring routine and some remained on the south side of the Tyne throughout the war and were even joined by some from London.

(opposite, top) Five months later, with what looks like the same working, No.60016 is passing the same location. Its external condition has taken a turn for the worse and that same grubby appearance was to become something of a 'trademark' for Gateshead's finest during the final years of steam on the ECML.

(opposite, bottom) We have now moved forward nearly five years to May 1964. SILVER KING'S fortunes have changed dramatically during the intervening period from when we last saw it performing at York. Heading the Up *POSTAL*, the Pacific is leaving Perth with the evening working. Allocated now to Ferryhill shed in Aberdeen, the A4 is turned out nicely after finding a new lease of life working over former Caledonian main lines, hauling trains such as this and the 3-hour expresses between the Granite City and Glasgow.

60017

Built: Doncaster, No.1823.

Put into traffic: 18th December 1935.

Original number: 2512.

Subsequent numbers:
    17 27th September 1946.
60017 27th April 1949.

Name: SILVER FOX.

Livery details:
Silver Grey unlined: 18th December 1935 to 27th September 1937.
Garter Blue with red and white lining: 6th November 1937 to 6th October 1941.
Black unlined: 22nd November 1941 to 4th August 1947.
Garter Blue with red and white lining: 25th September 1947 to 1st August 1950.
Dark Blue with black and white lining: 21st September 1950 to 19th November 1952.
Brunswick Green with orange and black lining: 21st December 1952 to breaking up.

Side skirting removed: 22nd November 1941.

Double chimney fitted: 18th May 1957.

Last major overhaul completed: 12th April 1962 General - Doncaster.

Last shed: New England from 16th June 1963.

Condemned: 20th October 1963.

Subsequent fate: Entered Doncaster Works 5th December 1963 for breaking up.

Comment: *The last of the initial four A4s, it too was cut up at Doncaster without a thought to its historical introduction and pre-war operation. King's Cross shed kept hold of this engine from its entry into traffic until the shed closed in 1963.*

(above) The last of the pioneering 1935 batch, No.60017 SILVER FOX spent the whole of its life allocated to King's Cross until that shed closed in June 1963. Seen passing Stoke summit and leaving behind the four track section, the immaculate Pacific is heading a Down afternoon train in September 1962. It's home shed have once again turned out one of their A4s in ex-works condition even though the last, and final, repaint the locomotive received was some five months previously.

(opposite, top) Passing Gamston signal box in June 1960, No.60017 has charge of a King's Cross bound express.

(opposite, bottom) Making a rather steamy southbound departure from Retford in February 1962, No.60017 was only days away from running back to Doncaster for its final major overhaul.

No.60017 makes yet another steamy departure, this time from a Doncaster stop whilst working an afternoon Leeds-King's Cross express in October 1962. An A1 stands by in the usual location as main line pilot. *(below)* April 1961 and SILVER FOX charges through Tuxford with an Up express. This view, captured from the bridge which carried the former Lancashire, Derbyshire & East Coast Railway main line over the ECML, shows the near empty sidings located at this once important junction which, like this A4, no longer exists.

(above) This is No.60023 GOLDEN EAGLE in June 1963 honest! Working a Down Newcastle express, the Gateshead A4 has not had the benefit of a 'Top Shed' clean this time because 34A was no more, its engines either withdrawn or dispersed to New England shed to lie idle awaiting their turn to be condemned. No such thing was going to happen to this A4 in the short term and by the end of the summer timetable it was transferred from Tyneside to Edinburgh before a further transfer during the following May took it to Aberdeen.

60023

Built: Doncaster, No.1847.

Put into traffic: 22nd December 1936.

Original number: 4482.

Subsequent numbers:
    23 22nd November 1946.
60023 25th March 1948.

Name: GOLDEN EAGLE.

Livery details:
LNER Green with black and white lining: 22nd December 1936 to 28th December 1937.
Garter Blue with red and white lining: 29th January 1938 to 31st July 1943.
Black unlined: 10th September 1943 to 15th August 1946.
Garter Blue with red and white lining: 28th September 1946 to 18th July 1949.
Dark Blue with black and white lining: 31st August 1949 to 6th August 1952.
Brunswick Green with orange and black lining: 4th September 1952 to breaking up.

Side skirting removed: 26th July 1941.

Double chimney fitted: 18th September 1958.

Last major overhaul completed: 10th January 1963 General - Doncaster.

Last shed: Aberdeen Ferryhill from 17th May 1964.

Condemned: 30th October 1964.

Subsequent fate: Sold for scrap to Motherwell Machinery & Scrap Co., Wishaw, in December 1964.

Comment: *The first A4 to enter traffic in the LNER standard green and lined livery. Lost its corridor tender No.5323 - in July 1941 when it was swapped for non-corridor type No.5667 from No.4462.*

Remember those days spotting from every vantage point and trying not to be noticed by authority? On a sunny evening in August 1959 (remember those too?) No.60023 runs over the flat crossing and into the station at Retford with a Down stopping express. *(below)* What's this? A clean Gateshead engine!? No.60023 GOLDEN EAGLE leaves behind the short tunnel at Askham with a Newcastle-London express in June 1960. The mystery behind the smart finish can be explained by the fact that the A4 had just completed a General overhaul days beforehand.

Before it sets, the low winter sun of a January afternoon in 1963 generates just enough light to bathe this pair of A4s at Doncaster shed. Nearest is No.60023 which has just completed a General but has yet to be released to traffic. To the left, standing on the works acceptance lines is No.60028 WALTER K.WHIGHAM which has just arrived from King's Cross shed having been condemned on 29th December last. The external condition of No.60028 is still a credit to 'Top Shed' who, right up to the end, kept the A4 immaculate. The weather at this time was cold, very cold, and it was set to get colder as one of the worst winters on record got a grip of the country. (below) Fast forward twenty months and three hundred or so miles northward and we find GOLDEN EAGLE on the turntable at Perth shed on a sunny morning in September 1964. Its external condition is what one might expect at this stage in the history of BR steam unkempt. Based now at Aberdeen, the A4 would be condemned at the end of October and sold for scrap by Christmas. This picture shows the new motive power, in the left background, stood alongside their fuel source whilst No.60023 stands next to its supply.

60024

Built: Doncaster, No.1848.

Put into traffic: 26th December 1936.

Original number: 4483.

Subsequent numbers:
585 30th March 1946.
  24 5th May 1946.
60024 18th June 1948.

Name: KINGFISHER.

Livery details:
LNER Green with black and white lining: 26th December 1936 to 30th November 1937.
Garter Blue with red and white lining: 7th January 1938 to 29th December 1942.
Black unlined: 4th February 1943 to 9th July 1946.
Garter Blue with red and white lining: 31st August 1946 to 31st May 1948.
BR Trial Purple: 18th June 1948 to 22nd July 1950.
Dark Blue with black and white lining: 24th August 1950 to 7th February 1952.
Brunswick Green with orange and black lining: 12th March 1952 to breaking up.

Side skirting removed: 6th November 1941.

Double chimney fitted: 20th August 1958.

Last major overhaul completed: 5th September 1964 Heavy Intermediate - Darlington.

Last shed: Aberdeen Ferryhill from 21st March 1965 (not made official until 6th May).

Condemned: 5th September 1966.

Subsequent fate: Sold for scrap to Hughes, Bolckow, North Blyth, October 1966.

Comment: *This engine's last four sheds were all located in Scotland Haymarket, Dalry Road, St Margarets, and Aberdeen Ferryhill.*

(above) Not long out from a 'General' at Doncaster (24th April to 15th June), Haymarket A4 No.60024 KINGFISHER runs down Gamston straight with the Saturdays Only service of *THE ELIZABETHAN* from King's Cross to Edinburgh on a warm morning in August 1961. A speed indicator was fitted during that overhaul, the last modification most of the class enjoyed before withdrawal. Note the plaque above the centre driving wheels which was fitted in July 1955.

(opposite, top) Nearly there! No.60024 runs through Hadley Wood on the approaches to London with the Up working of *THE ELIZABETHAN* in August 1961. This was to be the final season of running for this non-stop. The last Up service was run on 8th September 1961, hauled from Edinburgh by No.60009; none other than No.60022 worked the Down train. Haymarket shed provided three of their A4s as regulars on this train and beside 60009 and 60024, No.60031 was the other. Six and a half hours was the normal journey time each way.

(opposite, bottom) Taking on a new lease of life when allocated to Aberdeen in May 1965, No.60024 was kept in good external and internal condition by the staff at Ferryhill shed. A Heavy Intermediate overhaul at Darlington shops in 1964 considerably helped the Pacific to stretch its legs more than most into the middle of that last decade. Here in July 1966 the A4 was working an AberdeenGlasgow express through the woods at Cumbernauld. At the end of the summer timetable it was condemned and sold for scrap.

Shortly after its transfer to Ferryhill shed, KINGFISHER is seen in the company of V2 No.60919 at Perth shed in June 1965.

No.60024 in its element and, apparently, steam-tight. Coasting down the bank towards Dunblane, the immaculate 'fishing bird' heads the afternoon Aberdeen-Glasgow express in September 1965. At withdrawal, this A4 was three months shy of its thirtieth birthday.

(above) No.60025 FALCON, one of the 'Top Shed' favourites, has just breasted Stoke summit south of Grantham and is heading through the cutting with an express for King's Cross in August 1962. Considering the A4 has only been in traffic for two months since its last 'General', its external appearance isn't what we have come to expect from 34A.

60025

Built: Doncaster, No.1849.

Put into traffic: 23rd January 1937.

Original number: 4484.

Subsequent numbers:
  25 4th May 1946.
60025 27th January 1950.

Name: FALCON.

Livery details:
LNER Green with black and white lining: 23rd January 1937 to 11th November 1937.
Garter Blue with red and white lining: 18th December 1937 to 17th October 1941.
Black unlined: 30th November 1941 to 21st November 1947.
Garter Blue with red and white lining: 31st December 1947 to 16th December 1949.
Dark Blue with black and white lining: 27th January 1950 to 3rd November 1952.
Brunswick Green with orange and black lining: 6th December 1952 to breaking up.

Side skirting removed: 30th November 1941.

Double chimney fitted: 4th September 1958.

Last major overhaul completed: 20th June 1962 General - Doncaster.

Last shed: New England from 16th June 1963.

Condemned: 20th October 1963.

Subsequent fate: Entered Doncaster Works for cutting up 4th January 1964.

Comment: *Should have been renumbered 586 under the Thompson scheme on 31st March 1946 but was in Doncaster shops at the time (25th March to 4th May 1946) so although allocated, the number was not applied and the A4 emerged as No.25.*

A cold day in March 1962 makes for lots of steam as No.60025 heads south out of Retford with an Up express. *(below)* The Sunday diversions which took the expresses off their normal course along the ECML and via Gainsborough did not just run through that town, some used to stop there too. In February 1960 the crew of FALCON peer back along their train to await the guards signal prior to departure from Lea Road station with this Down express. Note that a speed indicator has yet to be fitted but that particular piece of equipment would be put on at the next General overhaul in a few months hence (5th May to 16th June). Lea Road station was built on the GGR/GNR Joint line and opened in 1867; it is still in business today.

In late March 1960, and with spring in the air, FALCON nears Eaton Wood whilst heading an afternoon express for London. The trailing smoke gives a good impression of the speed being achieved by the Pacific. *(below)* Approaching Grantham in September 1962, No.60025 has charge of late afternoon Down express. With the coming of the main line diesels, work for the King's Cross A4s was being lost at an alarming rate. The forthcoming winter of extremes would, in effect, give some of them a few months respite from the inevitable which was looming. June of 1963 would see their home shed closed and the remaining A4s transferred to New England where most went into storage with little or no hope of reprieve from withdrawal. The locomotive works at Doncaster was still scrapping steam locomotives in 1963 and it was to that place where most of the former 34A 'Streaks' ended up the place where they were all built.

60026

Built: Doncaster, No.1850.

Put into traffic: 20th February 1937.

Original number: 4485.

Subsequent numbers:
  587 18th April 1946.
   26 26th May 1946.
  60026 23rd September 1949.

Names:
KESTREL until 19th September 1947.
MILES BEEVOR from 1st November 1947.

Livery details:
LNER Green with black and white lining: 20th February 1937 to 29th October 1937.
Garter Blue with red and white lining: 8th December 1937 to 1st December 1941.
Black unlined: 18th January 1942 to 19th September 1947.
Garter Blue with red and white lining: 1st November 1947 to 11th August 1949.
Dark Blue with black and white lining: 23rd September 1949 to 29th September 1952.
Brunswick Green with orange and black lining: 24th October 1952 to breaking up.

Side skirting removed: 18th January 1942.

Double chimney fitted: 15th August 1957.

Last major overhaul completed: 1st August 1962 General - Doncaster.

Last shed: Aberdeen Ferryhill from 13th April 1964.

Condemned: 21st December 1965.

Subsequent fate: Sold for scrap to Hughes, Bolckow, North Blyth, in September 1967.

Comment: *Condemned at Perth after failing, No.60026 was initially sold for scrap to Motherwell Machinery & Scrap Co. in February 1966. However, the sale was cancelled at the 11th hour and the engine returned to Perth on 2nd August 1966. By the end of September it was in the works at Crewe in order to provide parts which were removed and used on preserved sister No.60007. The hulk was them sold for scrap.*

(above) Surprisingly, this scene at York Holgate is not dated in 1963 or '64 but during an October morning in 1959. No.60026 MILES BEEVOR has charge of the Up 'Scotch Goods' a well established fitted freight train which ran daily and moved goods fairly quickly over the long distances between London and Edinburgh. A4s had been used on this working from a period just before WWII and they became regulars with King's Cross supplying the motive power. The Down train left King's Cross goods depot in late afternoon. As can be seen the train consists a fairly mixed bag but nevertheless it was an important revenue earner of the LNER and BR. Note that the A4 has burnished buffers and drawgear which incidentally had nothing to do with any occasion nor was the Pacific ex-shops it was just the way 'Top Shed' treated their A4s at this period. Goods today, non-stop tomorrow!

(opposite, top) Passing Peppercorn A1 No.60119, which is stopped in the loop at Gamston, No.60026 rushes by with the Up working of *THE FLYING SCOTSMAN* in June 1960. The A4 is in fact wearing a headboard which was quite a rare occurrence for this express at that time.

(opposite, bottom) Ready for the dash to the south with an evening express, MILES BEEVOR whistles for the road at Grantham in July 1959. Even though No.60026 MILES BEEVOR was scrapped in North Blyth in 1967, the driving wheels seen in this view of the engine survive to this day and are fitted to sister No.60007 SIR NIGEL GRESLEY after a last minute change around at Crewe works in 1966.

With blossom on the trees above, No.60026 emerges from Stoke tunnel in May 1960 with an express for Newcastle. *(below)* From one iconic location to another: Some four summers have passed since the last image was recorded and by now our A4 Pacific has found a new home in Aberdeen. It is June 1964 and No.60026 is seen working home through Hilton Junction, just to the south of Perth, with a Glasgow-Aberdeen express.

(above) No.60027 MERLIN was one of the A4s which spent all of its life allocated to sheds in Scotland, Haymarket for 25-years, St Rollox for just over two, and one year all but three days back in Edinburgh but at St Margarets. Here in May 1964 the Pacific is departing from Perth with a morning service of the Glasgow to Aberdeen express. Note the naval plaque, which was attached in May 1946, still adorns the streamlined casing.

60027

Built: Doncaster, No.1851.

Put into traffic: 13th March 1937.

Original number: 4486.

Subsequent numbers:
   588 31st March 1946.
    27 5th May 1946.
   E27 11th March 1948.
60027 2nd June 1948.

Name: MERLIN.

Livery details:
LNER Green with black and white lining: 13th March 1937 to 11th November 1937.
Garter Blue with red and white lining: 18th December 1937 to 14th November 1941.
Black unlined: 27th December 1941 to 16th December 1946.
Garter Blue with red and white lining: 25th January 1947 to 21st May 1948.
BR Trial Purple: 2nd June 1948 to 16th May 1950.
Dark Blue with black and white lining: 7th July 1950 to 29th April 1952.
Brunswick Green with orange and black lining: 6th June 1952 to breaking up.

Side skirting removed: 27th December 1941.

Double chimney fitted: 12th February 1958.

Last major overhaul completed: 18th January 1962 General - Doncaster.

Last shed: St Margarets from 6th September 1964.

Condemned: 3rd September 1965.

Subsequent fate: Sold for scrap to G.H.Campbell, Shieldhall, in December 1965.

Comment: *Although a regular and popular performer on the expresses from Edinburgh right through to London, this engine spent the whole of its life allocated to sheds solely in Scotland Haymarket (25 years, 2 months), St Rollox (2 years, 3 months), and St Margarets (11 months, 3 weeks, 3 days) in that order.*

Pre-war, MERLIN was employed on the non-stops between the two capital cities and once hostilities had ceased, the A4 was once again a regular on the non-stop expresses introduced by British Railways. On a glorious June Sunday in 1960 No.60027 was captured at Eaton Wood working to King's Cross with the Sunday version of *THE ELIZABETHAN*, non-stop between Edinburgh and London. It had recently been ex-works where both AWS and a speed indicator were fitted. *(below)* During its final months of life at St Margarets shed, the A4 was employed on all sorts of work and here at Newcastleton on the Waverley route in June 1965 it has charge of a Carlisle to Edinburgh special. With apparent steam to spare as it tackles the climb, the grubby Pacific has just passed a diesel powered Up service.

Approaching the camera with a sound akin to a well maintained sowing machine, No.60027 MERLIN is passing J72 No.68677 which was shunting carriage stock at Clifton sidings on the northern approach to York station in August 1959. The train is, once again, *THE ELIZABETHAN* but with the headboard reversed. Haymarket, it will be noted, could turn out their A4s looking just like the King's Cross examples. *(below)* Back to the Waverley route in June 1965, MERLIN was captured running down grade past the burn at Whitrope. The placing of a diagonal warning stripe on the cab side sheets must have been organised by a pure optimist because the chances of this engine working 'under the wires' south of Crewe were essentially Nil! Condemned at the end of the summer timetable, No.60027 was shortly afterwards sold for scrap.

60028

Built: Doncaster, No.1852.

Put into traffic: 20th March 1937.

Original number: 4487.

Subsequent numbers:
    28 20th November 1946.
60028 7th June 1948.

Names:
SEA EAGLE until 9th August 1947.
WALTER K.WHIGHAM from 1st October 1947.

Livery details:
LNER Green with black and white lining: 20th March 1937 to 3rd January 1938.
Garter Blue with red and white lining: 12th February 1938 to 22nd September 1941.
Black unlined: 22nd November 1941 to 9th August 1947.
Garter Blue with red and white lining: 1st October 1947 to 24th May 1948.
BR Trial Purple: 7th June 1948 to 11th September 1950.
Dark Blue with black and white lining: 13th October 1950 to 21st January 1952.
Brunswick Green with orange and black lining: 22nd February 1952 to breaking up.

Side skirting removed: 5th July 1941.

Double chimney fitted: 2nd November 1957.

Last major overhaul completed: 18th April 1961 General - Doncaster.

Last shed: King's Cross from 23rd May 1948.

Condemned: 29th December 1962.

Subsequent fate: Entered Doncaster Works for cutting up 18th January 1963.

Comment: The first to have the side skirting removed to aid wartime maintenance.

(above) No.60028 WALTER K.WHIGHAM served at all of the ECML sheds which had an allocation of A4s prior to the ending of normal usage in 1963 Haymarket, Gateshead, Doncaster, Grantham, and King's Cross. It was from the latter shed that Pacific worked during BR days and in late August 1962, when the A4 was photographed south of Grantham with a Down express. The condition of No.60028, compared with its turnout just over a year before, leaves a lot to be desired; on 8th June 1961 it was chosen as the motive power for the Royal Train which took the Queen and her personal guests to the wedding of the Duke of Kent at York Minster.

(opposite, top) During a more certain period in its life, No.60028 is speeding south of Retford and nearing the summit at Markham Moor with an Up express in early March 1960.

(opposite, bottom) Early August 1962 and No.60028 runs through the cutting on the approach to Stoke tunnel with an express for King's Cross.

Leaning to the super-elevated curve, and giving off nice exhaust No.60028 runs past Gamston signal box with an Up express in May 1960. Some two years and seven months after this scene was recorded, the A4 was condemned, an early casualty of the inevitable decline of steam haulage on the ECML.

Just three months before condemnation, No.60028 WALTER K.WHIGHAM named after the LNER's last deputy Chairman works another Newcastle express northbound through the cutting at Saltersford, south of Grantham.

(above) Pristine after nearly four months on works receiving its final General overhaul, No.60009 UNION OF SOUTH AFRICA stands ready for trials on Doncaster shed yard on the afternoon of Thursday 7th November 1963. It is now coupled to corridor tender No.5332 which had stood spare at Doncaster Works since No.60033 had been taken in for scrapping during the previous January. No.5332 was one of the original ten 1928-built 8-wheel corridor tenders made for the A3s which were about to work the first LNER non-stop trains between London and Edinburgh. Three of that 1928 tender batch managed to reach preservation (*see also* page 94), including this one, although not with No.60009.

60009

Built: Doncaster, No.1853.

Put into traffic: 29th June 1937.

Original number: 4488.

Subsequent numbers:
    9 12th January 1947.
60009 5th May 1948.

Names:
OSPREY when ex-Erecting shop, 17th April 1937 to Paint shop.
UNION OF SOUTH AFRICA from 28th June 1937.

Livery details:
Garter Blue with red and white lining: 19th April 1937 to 31st January 1942.
Black unlined: 21st March 1942 to 14th January 1947.
Garter Blue with red and white lining: 21st February 1947 to 16th June 1949.
Dark Blue with black and white lining: 4th August 1949 to 21st August 1952.
Brunswick Green with orange and black lining: 2nd October 1952 to sale.

Side skirting removed: 21st March 1942.

Double chimney fitted: 18th November 1958.

Last major overhaul completed: 6th November 1963 General - Doncaster.

Last shed: Aberdeen Ferryhill from 20th May 1962.

Condemned: 1st June 1966.

Subsequent fate: Sold for preservation July 1966.

Comment: *This A4 was responsible for a couple of noteworthy 'lasts' insomuch as being the last of the class to have a major overhaul at Doncaster, and also the last steam locomotive to be given a General at that works. It was also the last A4 to work a train out of King's Cross terminus.*

Proudly displaying its 64B shedplate, No.60009 nears the signal box at Barrowby Road to the north of Grantham with an Edinburgh-King's Cross express in August 1961. Note the train headboard being returned to 'Top Shed'; stowing the board on the lamp iron was more logical than keeping it in the cab where its presence could be a nuisance at least.

A few days later, No.60009 is spotted returning the same headboard to 34A. This time the A4 is at Ganwick corner, approaching Hadley Wood north tunnel whilst the rear carriages of its train are still emerging from Potters Bar tunnel with an express from Edinburgh.

This A4 was the first one received by Ferryhill shed in Aberdeen and they were justly proud of it. Arriving 20th May 1962, it served the depot for four years prior to withdrawal. In June 1964, halfway through its tenure at 61B, No.60009 runs the morning Aberdeen-Glasgow express out of Perth on its way to Buchanan Street. No doubt about it, that late 'General' at Doncaster certainly prolonged its life, but the care and maintenance provided at the Aberdeen shed helped also.

On Saturday 24th October 1964, UNION OF SOUTH AFRICA worked the *JUBILEE REQUIEM* special, a joint venture between the RCTS and SLS, from King's Cross to Newcastle. Here in glorious sunshine the train is passing BOCM just north of Selby. Although we did not know at that time, events such as this were to become the future for this engine.

60010

Built: Doncaster, No.1854.

Put into traffic: 4th May 1937 for trials.

Original number: 4489.

Subsequent numbers:
10 10th May 1946.
60010 27th October 1948.

Names:
WOODCOCK to 17th May 1937 to Paint shop.
DOMINION OF CANADA from 15th June 1937.

Livery details:
Shop grey: 4th to 17th May 1937.
Garter Blue with red and white lining: 24th May 1937 to 9th January 1942.
Black unlined: 21st February 1942 to 15th October 1947.
Garter Blue with red and white lining: 20th November 1947 to 21st August 1950.
Dark Blue with black and white lining: 29th September 1950 to 3rd April 1952.
Brunswick Green with orange and black lining: 8th May 1952 to preservation.

Side skirting removed: 21st February 1942.

Double chimney fitted: 27th December 1957.

Last major overhaul completed: 5th December 1962 General - Doncaster.

Last shed: Aberdeen Ferryhill from 20th October 1963.

Condemned: 29th May 1965.

Subsequent fate: Preserved in Canada but returned to UK in time for 2013 celebrations at York.

Comment: The second of the 1937 batch to lose the original 'bird' name in favour of a name with an Empire theme.

(above) On Sunday 16th December 1962, No.60010 DOMINION OF CANADA stands on the works reception lines at Doncaster shed awaiting entry into 'The Plant' for a Non-Classified repair. At this time the A4 was allocated to King's Cross depot and some of the clean external condition associated with that shed is still evident. This short visit to main works was not going to be the last for the Pacific. On 20th May 1963 it went into Doncaster again for a month long Casual Light repair. This was followed by a Non-Classified repair carried out at Inverurie in May 1964, and finally a supposed entry into Darlington shops on 12th May 1965 which was not carried out and so the locomotive languished in open air storage at Darlington Bank Top engine shed until it was finally sent to Crewe for cosmetic repairs in August 1966. It was finally shipped to Canada for preservation on 19th April 1967 and that was finally that! Or so it seemed.

(opposite, top) On a sunny August morning in 1962 No.60010 descends the bank at Great Ponton, just south of Grantham, with an express for the north.

(opposite, bottom) Back at one of our photographer's favourite locations near the River Idle, we see No.60010 leaving Retford behind as it strides out for London in 1961. One of the interesting entries in Darlington Works records unearthed by W.B.Yeadon about this locomotive, concerns its time at Darlington in 1965: The record states 'For sale to be scrapped - 5th July 1965'. A close shave then!

The eighteen months spent in Scotland at the end of its career, saw No.60010 allocated to Ferryhill shed from where it worked the expresses to and from Aberdeen to Glasgow. In June 1964 the A4 is waiting at the north end of Perth station for the 'right-away' with a Glasgow-Aberdeen express.

With twelve on, DOMINION OF CANADA seems to be making light work with a southbound express whilst climbing Gamston bank in September 1960.

(above) No.60011 EMPIRE OF INDIA stands on the shed yard at Leeds Holbeck on 25th March 1963 after working into the city via the Settle & Carlisle line with an overnight sleeper from Edinburgh. Not the normal motive power for the train or the route either. However, the diesel locomotive rostered to haul the train had failed in Edinburgh and the former Haymarket A4, actually visiting from Aberdeen, was seconded for the job. From Holbeck the Pacific went light engine to York before returning north on an unknown working. Looking at the external condition of No.60011, it is difficult to comprehend that it was once one of 64B's favourites'. *Courtesy Gavin Morrison.*

60011

Built: Doncaster, No.1855.

Put into traffic: 25th June 1937.

Original number: 4490.

Subsequent numbers:
    11 23rd November 1946.
60011 17th March 1949.

Name: EMPIRE OF INDIA.

Livery details:
Garter Blue with red and white lining: 15th May 1937 to 10th September 1942.
Black unlined: 22nd October 1942 to 26th October 1946.
Garter Blue with red and white lining: 30th November 1946 to 26th April 1950.
Dark Blue with black and white lining: 8th June 1950 to 11th March 1952.
Brunswick Green with orange and black lining: 10th April 1952 to breaking up.

Side skirting removed: 1st November 1941.

Double chimney fitted: 11th January 1958.

Last major overhaul completed: 30th May 1962 General - Doncaster.

Last shed: Aberdeen Ferryhill from 11th June 1962.

Condemned: 11th May 1964.

Subsequent fate: Cut up at Darlington Works after failing an examination in May 1964.

Comment: *The second of the 1937 batch to lose the original 'bird' name in favour of a name with an Empire theme.*

(above) A summer idyll! Haymarket's No.60012 COMMONWEALTH OF AUSTALIA (the equal longest nameplate in the class) is about to cross the River Idle at Retford with the northbound working of *THE ELIZABETHAN* in August 1958. This was the way to spend those school holidays.

(opposite, top) Released from 'The Plant' works on the last Friday of October 1960, after a six-week long General overhaul (13th September to 28th October), No.60011 rests on shed at Doncaster on Sunday 6th November following a week of running-in. That week on the road, and the nights spent on shed at 36A, have taken their toll on the ex-works sheen which has disappeared beneath a thin blanket of soot and grime. No problem though because when Haymarket eventually got it back, they soon had it polished up to that 'just out of the paint shop' look. *Courtesy Gavin Morrison.*

(opposite, bottom) Another of the class to work from Aberdeen, No.60011 is seen on Ferryhill shed yard in May 1963. Like No.60010, this Pacific also ended up with one of the 1928-built corridor tenders which had served Gresley's A3s for nearly nine years before their transfer to A4 class. This is tender No.5328 which though coupled to EMPIRE OF INDIA in October 1960, had actually been attached to the Pacific before when the A4 was put into traffic in June 1937. Both locomotive and tender were cut up together at Darlington Works.

60012

Built: Doncaster, No.1855.

Put into traffic: 22nd June 1937.

Original number: 4491.

Subsequent numbers:
   12 12th January 1947.
60012 26th May 1948.

Name: COMMONWEALTH OF AUSTRALIA.

Livery details:
Garter Blue with red and white lining: 15th May 1937 to 1st August 1942.
Black unlined: 12th September 1942 to 25th June 1947.
Garter Blue with red and white lining: 9th August 1947 to 12th July 1949.
Dark Blue with black and white lining: 24th August 1949 to 21st October 1952.
Brunswick Green with orange and black lining: 21st November 1952 to breaking up.

Side skirting removed: 12th September 1942.

Double chimney fitted: 18th July 1958.

Last major overhaul completed: 27th October 1961 General - Doncaster.

Last shed: Aberdeen Ferryhill from 20th January 1964.

Condemned: 20th August 1964.

Subsequent fate: Sold for scrap to Motherwell Machinery & Scrap Co., Wishaw in March 1965.

Comment: *Another Haymarket based engine which was a frequent visitor to King's Cross having hauled many of the non-stop trains from and back to Edinburgh, before and after WWII.*

Having transferred to Aberdeen in January 1964, via the ex Caley shed at Dalry Road, No.60012 found reason to visit Edinburgh in June 1964 and is at Inverkeithing whistling for the road onto the Forth Bridge. Just weeks later the A4 was condemned and after spending the following winter waiting for a buyer, it was sold for scrap in March '65.

(above) No.60013 DOMINION OF NEW ZEALAND (the other 'longest' nameplate) nears Retford crossing on an August evening in 1961 with the Down *TEES-TYNE PULLMAN*. The speed indicator had been fitted at the last 'General' in June whilst the electrification warning signs are new. Allocated to King's Cross shed for much of its life, this A4 was coupled to a corridor tender No.5647 which was different from the others in that all four axles had been fitted with Hoffman roller bearings in 1939.

(opposite) It is the end of October 1961. It is bright and sunny but cold. From the north comes the sound of a chime whistle and in the distance can be seen a cloud of steam issuing from a small black oblong. Suddenly the black oblong is not so small and before you know it, a flash of green, followed by maroon, with lots of steam passing overhead and around you and quickly dispersed by the easterly wind as another black oblong recedes towards the south just as fast as the first one came from the north. No.60013, living up to the magic created by a speeding A4, working hard against a stiff wind on a cold day, just south of Retford. This engine's chime whistle was different from the rest of the class because it was one presented by the New Zealand Government in 1938; their version had five notes of lower pitch and a lesser degree of musical tone.

60013

Built: Doncaster, No.1857.

Put into traffic: 27th June 1937.

Original number: 4492.

Subsequent numbers:
    13 17th August 1946.
60013 20th May 1949.

Name: DOMINION OF NEW ZEALAND.

Livery details:
Garter Blue with red and white lining: 27th June 1937 to 23rd September 1941.
Black unlined: 21st November 1941 to 11th June 1946.
Garter Blue with red and white lining: 17th August 1946 to 5th April 1949.
Dark Blue with black and white lining: 20th May 1949 to 26th August 1952.
Brunswick Green with orange and black lining: 8th October 1952 to breaking up.

Side skirting removed: 21st November 1941.

Double chimney fitted: 4th July 1958.

Last major overhaul completed: 29th June 1961 General - Doncaster.

Last shed: King's Cross from 4th June 1950.

Condemned: 18th April 1963.

Subsequent fate: Entered Doncaster Works for breaking up 23rd April 1963.

Comment: *This A4 was fitted with a five-note chime whistle which had been presented by the New Zealand Government Railway to the LNER prior to WWII; the whistle had a lower pitch and was apparently less musical than the LNER chime type. Whatever happened to that whistle?*

Running through Hatfield in July 1961, No.60013 has charge of a King's Cross express.

With the unmistakable skyline of York receding in the distance, No.60013 accelerates away from the city with a Newcastle-London express in August 1959.

Having just breasted the summit at Markham Moor, No.60013, and its southbound express, pick up speed over the descending stretch in late March 1962. The A4 had recently been in works for a minor repair Casual Light which had taken nearly six weeks to complete but most of that time was actually spent waiting in the works yard. Note the slipping standards of cleanliness creeping in at 34A.

With a Newcastle-King's Cross express in tow, No.60013 passes Leeman Road on the approach into York in September 1959. All is well in the world of the A4s and although the diesels are starting to encroach from the west, the pride of the ECML motive power still reigns supreme.

60029

Built: Doncaster, No.1858.

Put into traffic: 26th July 1937.

Original number: 4493.

Subsequent numbers:
29 26th May 1946.
60029 16th July 1948.

Name: WOODCOCK.

Livery details:
LNER Green with black and white lining: 26th July 1937 to 10th June 1938.
Garter Blue with red and white lining: 25th July 1938 to 30th July 1942.
Black unlined: 11th September 1942 to 1st May 1947.
Garter Blue with red and white lining: 4th June 1947 to 28th May 1948.
BR Trial Purple: 16th July 1948 to 28th November 1949.
Dark Blue with black and white lining: 13th January 1950 to 15th September 1952.
Brunswick Green with orange and black lining: 30th October 1952 to breaking up.

Side skirting removed: 11th September 1942.

Double chimney fitted: 3rd October 1958.

Last major overhaul completed: 13th December 1961 General - Doncaster.

Last shed: New England from 16th June 1963.

Condemned: 20th October 1963.

Subsequent fate: Entered Doncaster Works for cutting up 4th January 1964.

Comment: *Carrying the 'bird' name originally bestowed on No.4489, this engine was also given the LNER lined green but with the restoration of the more pleasing parabolic shaped curve of the green livery at the front end.*

(above) With storm clouds gathering, No.60029 WOODCOCK makes an effortless job running north past Markham Moor in 1962 with the eight vehicles of *THE HARROGATE SUNDAY PULLMAN*.

(opposite, top) It wasn't all non-stop running for the A4s. No.60029 is seen at the favoured location of Ordsall, south of Retford, as it lays down a nice smoke trail and accelerates away from the Retford stop with this stopping train to King's Cross in October 1961. The Pacific was due into works soon after this scene was recorded, for its final General overhaul although, at the time, it was just another 'General'.

(oppoite, bottom) Its wasn't very often that you saw an A4 shunting but this scene at Grantham, in May 1961, reveals No.60029 at the north end of the station marshalling e.c.s. from the Nottingham line side of the junction to the main line side, in order to make up the train for a Grantham to King's Cross 'stopper' which it then worked forward to London. Grantham shed played host to all of the King's Cross A4s and over the years had a number of them allocated, especially during the war years and immediately afterwards WOODCOCK, however, was not one of them.

Not long out from a 'General' at Doncaster, No.60029 looks rather smart prior to turning on the triangle at Grantham shed in May 1960. It was at that overhaul (26th February to 8th April 1960) that the speed indicator was fitted. The tenders in the left background are sludge carriers used to convey the resultant slurry left over from the water softening plant at the shed.

WOODCOCK again at Grantham shed but in June 1960.

(above) ANDREW K.McCOSH was the second name carried by No.60003 and was fitted to honour the Chairman of the LNER Locomotive Committee who also was one of only five Directors to serve the Company throughout its 25-year existence. On a delightful evening in May 1961 the immaculate A4 approaches Grantham with a heavy Down express, the driver no doubt making use of the newly acquired speed indicator fitted at the last overhaul. This engine was one of the early recipients of the British Railways ATC (Automatic Train Control) which later became AWS (Automatic Warning System) fitted as an experiment in April 1950. Before AWS was adopted totally by BR in the late 1950s, a number of the class were fitted during the mid-50s' to expand the 'experiment' on the East Coast main line.

60003

Built: Doncaster, No.1859.

Put into traffic: 12th August 1937.

Original number: 4494.

Subsequent numbers:
  3 11th September 1946.
60003 4th March 1949.

Names:
OSPREY until 11th July 1942.
ANDREW K.McCOSH from 21ST August 1942.

Livery details:
LNER Green with black and white lining: 12th August 1937 to 1st September 1938.
Garter Blue with red and white lining: 20th October 1938 to 11th July 1942.
Black unlined: 21st August 1942 to 17th May 1947.
Garter Blue with red and white lining: 21st June 1947 to 28th February 1950.
Dark Blue with black and white lining: 19th April 1950 to 3rd September 1951.
Brunswick Green with orange and black lining: 10th October 1951 to breaking up.

Side skirting removed: 21st August 1942.

Double chimney fitted: 5th July 1957.

Last major overhaul completed: 2nd February 1961 General - Doncaster.

Last shed: King's Cross 15th September 1957.

Condemned: 29th December 1962.

Subsequent fate: Entered Doncaster Works for cutting up 15th January 1963.

Comment: *Carrying from new, another of the discarded 'bird' names, No.4494 would itself change identity in wartime when it was named after one of the LNER Directors. The name OSPREY however lived on and was carried during BR days by Peppercorn A1 No.60131 from June 1950 until withdrawal in 1965. More of a Phoenix perhaps, the name was used again in 1990 when No.60009 (which had originally carried it for a couple of months in 1937) was adorned with the name so that it could take part in the Forth Bridge Centenary celebrations without its politically sensitive at the time 'country' name offending anyone.*

The morning sunshine bathes No.60003 and its Newcastle bound train near Hatfield in July 1961.

On a glorious afternoon In May 1959, No.60003 is captured working a Newcastle-King's Cross express on the approach to York. The double chimney was fitted during overhaul at Doncaster in June 1957.

No.60003 ANDREW K.McCOSH threads the cutting at Saltersford in August 1962 with an Up morning express for London. This is one of the King's Cross Pacifics and you can certainly tell the difference by its external appearance. By the 21st August a visit to works was necessary for some unknown reason but the repair was classified as Casual Light so may well have been the result of a collision of sorts or a mechanical failure which 'Top Shed' could not deal with; whatever it was took a month to deal with and may well have had some influence on the early withdrawal of this engine shortly after the following Christmas. *(below)* On a rather bright Sunday in February 1960, No.60003 made an appearance at Gainsborough and is seen approaching Lea Road station with a diverted King's Cross to Newcastle express. These Sunday diversions became a regular occurrence as engineering work on the ECML became more intense to not only upgrade the route for faster running but continually maintain the high speed main line. Note the chime whistle announcing the arrival.

60030

Built: Doncaster, No.1860.

Put into traffic: 30th August 1937.

Original number: 4495.

Subsequent numbers:
    30 23rd November 1946.
60030 30th July 1948.

Names:
GREAT SNIPE until 11th September 1937.
GOLDEN FLEECE from 25th September 1937.

Livery details:
LNER Green with black and white lining: 30th August 1937 to 11th September 1937.
Garter Blue with red and white lining: 25th September 1937 to 6th November 1941.
Black unlined: 20th December 1941 to 5th November 1946.
Garter Blue with red and white lining: 7th December 1946 to 26th September 1949.
Dark Blue with black and white lining: 10th November 1949 to 13th August 1952.
Brunswick Green with orange and black lining: 24th September 1952 to breaking up.

Side skirting removed: 20th December 1941.

Double chimney fitted: 15th May 1958.

Last major overhaul completed: 28th July 1961 General - Doncaster.

Last shed: King's Cross from 15th September 1957.

Condemned: 29th December 1962.

Subsequent fate: Entered Doncaster Works for cutting up 25th January 1963.

Comment: *The last of the A4 to carry green livery from new, this engine wore it for the shortest time of all less than two weeks before it was adorned with the Garter Blue worn by those hauling streamlined trains. The reason for this apparent wasteful exercise was to prepare No.4495 to haul the newly introduced WEST RIDING LIMITED, the third of the LNER's streamlined trains, which was to run between Leeds and London. Sister engines Nos.4496 and 4497 were designated originally for the job but the latter would not be ready for the inaugural runs, hence the promotion of our subject's fortunes. To further complicate matters, a new name, befitting the train's commercial customers' backgrounds, was bestowed on No.4495 prior to the first run.*

(above) Another favourite location, and in glorious autumn sunshine too! This time, No.60030 GOLDEN FLEECE accelerates north out of York, past Clifton locomotive shed, with *THE FLYING SCOTSMAN* in September 1959. This would be the lightweight (eleven vehicles) summer timetable non-stop train which was initially made famous by the A3s from 1928. Being the only class with corridor tenders in BR days, the A4s took on the mantle of working the summer service, along with the other non-stops. The corridor tender coupled to No.60030 at this time was No.5327, one of the original 1928 versions.

(opposite, top) Climbing out of Grantham with an Up express in August 1961, GOLDEN FLEECE is in ex-works condition.

(opposite, bottom) Taking its turn on the Down 'Scotch Goods' No.60030 runs through Grantham with clear signals in the late afternoon during a lovely day in May 1960. Recently ex-works from a Casual Light repair, the lower front end casing of the engine appears as though a fresh coat of paint has been applied.

Back on passenger express work and looking as resplendent as ever, GOLDEN FLEECE runs out of Peascliffe tunnel in July 1960 with an Up working.

With thirteen on, including dining and kitchen cars at the front, our A4 meanders into Gainsborough Lea Road with a diverted Down ECML express in May 1961. This was one of the A4s which spent much of the war and some years afterwards allocated to Grantham shed. It did a final stint at Grantham during the summer of 1957 but returned to King's Cross from where it was withdrawn on 29th December 1962 a rather dark day for the A4 class.

(above) No.60008 DWIGHT D.EISENHOWER runs over the River Idle near Retford on a perfect July day in 1961. Just like No.60030, this A4 also took up residency at Grantham from 7th April to 15th September 1957 for the duration of the summer timetable but that exercise was never repeated and King's Cross kept hold of its A4s until closure. Although transferred to New England with the others on 16th June 1963, No.60008 was withdrawn, rather than condemned, on the following 20th July whilst at Doncaster Works. Although refurbished cosmetically, the locomotive was not repaired and was shipped to the USA in its latest BR livery, as here.

60008

Built: Doncaster, No.1861.

Put into traffic: 4th September 1937.

Original number: 4496.

Subsequent numbers:
     8   23rd November 1946.
60008   29th October 1948.

Names:
GOLDEN SHUTTLE until 4th July 1945.
DWIGHT D.EISENHOWER from 25th September 1945.

Livery details:
Garter Blue with red and white lining: 4th September 1937 to 10th December 1941.
Black unlined: 30th January 1942 to 4th July 1945.
Garter Blue with red and white lining: 25th September 1945 to 2nd May 1950.
Dark Blue with black and white lining: 14th June 1950 to 9th October 1951.
Brunswick Green with orange and black lining: 9th November 1951 to preservation.

Side skirting removed: 30th January 1942.

Double chimney fitted: 20th August 1958.

Last major overhaul completed: 17th May 1962 General - Doncaster.

Last shed: New England from 16th June 1963.

Condemned (Withdrawn): 20th July 1963.

Subsequent fate: Entered Doncaster Works 19th July 1963 for restoration work but not repairs, prior to being shipped to the United States and preservation.

Comment: *Was it coincidental or just a fluke that No.4496 entered Doncaster shops on 4th July 1945 for a General overhaul and a change of name to that of the Supreme Allied Commander Europe Dwight D.Eisenhower. It was the first A4 to be restored from wartime black to the LNER Garter Blue livery.*

Obviously not a non-stop with that horsebox behind the tender but nevertheless quite a load for No.60008 passing Markham Moor with a Down express in March 1960. The Pacific is immaculate in every respect but it still went into shops in early May for a 'General' because these locomotives required constant care, not only by their sheds but also at main works. During its 25-year lifetime, No.60008 had no less than eighteen major overhauls and half as many minor repairs. Add to that eleven boiler changes and the cost of keeping them in first class condition starts to mount up quite steeply. *(below)* Another Grantham departure in August 1962 for No.60008, this time it's an early morning express for King's Cross, and seen from an unusual angle for this location.

No.60008 on the curve at Saltersford, south of Grantham, with an Up express, in August 1962; when four tracks existed here.

No.60008 was certainly busy in August 1962 and this illustration shows the Pacific passing High Dyke on the run up to Stoke tunnel with another Up express. The train originated at Newcastle and would have been worked by a Gateshead Pacific, or a V2 at this time of year, as far as Grantham where this King's Cross A4 would have taken over. Grantham was a principal locomotive changeover point, its allocation and visiting locomotives reflecting that fact; the event of changing engines here was basically hourly and had been a regular and long-standing operational procedure on the ECML from early Great Northern days the coming of the diesels was to change all of that, and much more!

60031

Built: Doncaster, No.1862.

Put into traffic: 2nd October 1937.

Original number: 4497.

Subsequent numbers:
31 30th May 1946.
60031 4th June 1948.

Name: GOLDEN PLOVER.

Livery details:
Garter Blue with red and white lining: 2nd October 1937 to 3rd April 1942.
Black unlined: 16th May 1942 to 16th June 1947.
Garter Blue with red and white lining: 1st August 1947 to 16th May 1949.
Dark Blue with black and white lining: 5th July 1949 to 11th June 1952.
Brunswick Green with orange and black lining: 23rd July 1952 to cutting up.

Side skirting removed: 16th May 1942.

Double chimney fitted: 11th March 1958.

Last major overhaul completed: 22nd August 1962 General - Doncaster.

Last shed: St Rollox from 3rd February 1962.

Condemned: 29th October 1965.

Subsequent fate: Sold for scrap to G.H.Campbell, Shieldhall, December 1965.

Comment: *Yet another A4 which spent the whole of its working life in Scotland. Firstly it was at Haymarket for 24 years and from where it took regular turns on many of the non-stop runs to London. Secondly, No.60031 spent its remaining three and a half years at the former Caledonian shed at St Rollox in Glasgow from where it worked mainly to Aberdeen on the 3-hour expresses.*

(above) No.60031 GOLDEN PLOVER passing the woods south of Hatfield with the London (King's Cross)-Edinburgh (Waverley) Saturdays Only version of *THE ELIZABETHAN* in August 1961. Haymarket based since new, this engine was a late receiver of the BR AWS equipment and was fitted as late as May 1960 during the general scheme to fit all locomotives eventually, starting with express passenger locomotives. Note that the Saturday service of this train was not a non-stop, the General Utility Van (GUV) between train and tender having no corridor connections for crew change.

(opposite, top) The Saturdays Only service of *THE ELIZABETHAN* again but this time its the Up train passing the Nottingham line junction at Grantham. The date is sometime in July 1961 and No.60031 looks magnificent in every respect. Note the nameplate has a pale blue background whereas black and red are the other colours used with the A4s. There did not appear to be a standard for background colours and some plates had changes from one to another colour during BR days (*see* elsewhere in this album).

It's that train again! GOLDEN PLOVER certainly was flavour of the month or so it seemed in July 1961. Here the A4 has the weekday non-stop Down working with the headboard turned so that all could see its name. The location is Gamston bank with the Pacific and train romping along. The A4s were intensively used during those final years of ECML steam workings and it was possible to see one particular A4 go north one day with a non-stop, south with the return working next day, and so on to the end of the week. Some members of the class clocked up six consecutive workings on *THE ELIZABETHAN* alone in 1961; add the other jobs undertaken which involved a stop or two and it is easy to appreciate just how important this class was to the operations of the ECML passenger, and goods, working.

(above) At an unknown date but certainly after April 1959, No.60007 SIR NIGEL GRESLEY stands in the throat of the shed yard at Grantham. It will be noted that the engine is carrying a reversed headboard denoting that it was either about to haul a named train, or had just come off such a working after being relieved at this place.

(opposite, top) Fresh from a 'General' No.60031 climbs Gamston bank near Eaton Wood in August 1959 with the Up Sunday service of THE ELIZABETHAN.

(opposite, bottom) As the 'Deltic' diesels arrived on the ECML the A4s were either withdrawn or transferred. No.60031 was one of those transferred, to, of all places the former Caledonian Railway depot at St Rollox in north Glasgow. The transfer took effect from 3rd February 1962 and enabled St Rollox shed to use the A4 on the accelerated 3-hour expresses to Aberdeen. In June 1965 however, No.60031 was working the morning Dundee to Glasgow express and is departing from Perth. As can be seen, the Glasgow depot did not hold the Pacific in the same reverence that Haymarket once did. Note also the cab stripe, a marking carried by No.60027 too. GOLDEN PLOVER was condemned at the end of October 1965 and sold for scrap.

60007

Built: Doncaster, No.1863.

Put into traffic: 30th October 1937.

Original number: 4498.

Subsequent numbers:
    7 12th January 1947.
60007 24th March 1948.

Name: SIR NIGEL GRESLEY.

Livery details:
Garter Blue with red and white lining: 30th October 1937 to 1st January 1942.
Black unlined: 21st February 1942 to 12th January 1947.
Garter Blue with red and white lining: 6th March 1947 to 11th August 1950.
Dark Blue with black and white lining: 27th September 1950 to 12th March 1952.
Brunswick Green with orange and black lining: 17th April 1952 to preservation.

Side skirting removed: 21st February 1942.

Double chimney fitted: 13th December 1957.

Last major overhaul completed: 25th October 1962 General - Doncaster.

Last shed: Aberdeen Ferryhill from 20th July 1964.

Condemned (Withdrawn): 1st February 1966.

Subsequent fate: Sold to A4 Preservation Society, May 1966.

Comment: *This locomotive was Gresley's one hundredth Pacific and the name bestowed upon it was suggested by a railway enthusiast. The LNER authorities heartily agreed to the naming and from that single act another A4 was to become the subject for preservation nearly thirty years later.*

Information regarding date or the location of this illustration was not forthcoming so all we can say is that No.60007 apparently has charge of the late afternoon Down working of the 'Scotch Goods' on a summer evening in Lincolnshire, after June 1959.

Leaving the very short Askham tunnel behind in May 1959, No.60007 runs south with an express made up of a fantastic variety of vehicles differing in livery, style and origin.

The northern end of Perth station in June 1965 SIR NIGEL is 'brewing up' prior to departure with the late afternoon Glasgow-Aberdeen express. The former King's Cross A4 got to its new home in Aberdeen via New England (16th June 1963), and St Margarets (20th October 1963), finally reaching Ferryhill on 20th July 1964. Without a doubt, the transfer of the A4s to the Aberdeen express services certainly had a bearing on the preservation, in working order, of so many of the class. Although BR had designated one for a museum and two others gifted to overseas countries, enthusiasts made sure that more would survive the BR annihilation of steam. And this is one of them. *(below)* No.60007 accelerates away from the Perth stop with an evening Glasgow to Aberdeen express in September 1965. These trains would often have a number of English enthusiasts aboard enjoying the thrill of A4 haulage once again after being deprived of such south of the border since 1964.

60004

Built: Doncaster, No.1864.

Put into traffic: 10th December 1937.

Original number: 4462.

Subsequent numbers:
    4 25th August 1946.
    E4 20th January 1948.
60004 25th May 1948.

Names:
GREAT SNIPE until 5th June 1941.
WILLIAM WHITELAW from 23rd July 1941.

Livery details:
Garter Blue with red and white lining: 10th December 1937 to 16th September 1942.
Black unlined: 31st October 1942 to 1st October 1946.
Garter Blue with red and white lining: 14th November 1946 to 10th July 1950.
Dark Blue with black and white lining: 10th August 1950 to 21st January 1952.
Brunswick Green with orange and black lining: 29th February 1952 to breaking up.

Side skirting removed: 23rd July 1941.

Double chimney fitted: 5th December 1957.

Last major overhaul completed: 31st December 1962 General - Doncaster.

Last shed: Aberdeen Ferryhill from 17th June 1963.

Condemned: 17th July 1966.

Subsequent fate: Sold for scrap to Motherwell Machinery & Scrap, Wishaw, October 1966.

Comment: *The first of the class to have the side skirting removed, Doncaster did not do the complete job though and left the portion in front of the cylinders intact. On transfer to Haymarket shed, direct from the works visit, the front skirting was removed completely and that then set the trend for the rest of the skirt removals.*

(above) One of the rarer A4s, at least as far as colour transparencies go. No.60004 started life as GREAT SNIPE but was renamed WILLIAM WHITELAW in July 1941. Although it worked the whole length of the ECML, it was shedded at most of the major sheds along that railway too. Unusually it had two stints at Aberdeen Ferryhill, the first when Haymarket gave it up on 11th June 1962 but recalled it at the end of that summer's timetable. Eventually, on 17th June 1963 it took up permanent residency at 61B and it was from there that it was working when captured by the camera at Perth in June 1964 with a Glasgow bound express. Condemned on 17th July 1966, No.60004 was later sold for scrap.

(opposite, top) On 19th September 1965 No.60004 was called upon to work an RCTS West Riding branch enthusiasts' special *THE BLYTH AND TYNE RAIL TOUR* from Leeds, and here at Eaglescliffe near Stockton it has paused for photographic purposes. Apparently the Pacific gave a good account of itself on the return journey averaging 72 m.p.h. on the racetrack between Darlington and York. *Courtesy Gavin Morrison.*

(opposite, bottom) The view from the footplate of No.60004 at Northallerton, on the outward leg of the aforementioned rail tour. *Courtesy Gavin Morrison.*

60018

Built: Doncaster, No.1865.

Put into traffic: 27th November 1937.

Original number: 4463.

Subsequent numbers:
    18 15th September 1946.
60018 16th October 1948.

Name: SPARROW HAWK.

Livery details:
Garter Blue with red and white lining: 27th November 1937 to 14th July 1943.
Black unlined: 22nd August 1943 to 20th November 1946.
Garter Blue with red and white lining: 28th December 1946 to 23rd January 1950.
Dark Blue with black and white lining: 5th April 1950 to 28th August 1951.
Brunswick Green with orange and black lining: 4th October 1951 to breaking up.

Side skirting removed: 1st November 1941.

Double chimney fitted: 5th October 1957.

Last major overhaul completed: 17th February 1961 General - Doncaster.

Last shed: Gateshead from 3rd November 1945.

Condemned: 19th June 1963.

Subsequent fate: Entered Doncaster Works for cutting up 10th July 1963.

Comment: *This A4 spent all of its life allocated to sheds on Tyneside Gateshead and Heaton, most of the war years at the latter establishment.*

(above) A Tyneside A4 through and through, No.60018 SPARROW HAWK spent its whole life working from either Gateshead or Heaton sheds. In July 1961 it was allocated to the former establishment but you would be hard pressed to say so because, for once, it was cleanish! Approaching Barrowby Road at Grantham, the A4 has a Down Newcastle express in tow, the first two vehicles of which are an articulated set. The Speed indicator was fitted during the engine's last 'General' at Doncaster.

(opposite, top) Four months earlier, in March 1961, No.60018 was photographed at Markham Moor with an Up Newcastle express which it worked as far as Grantham. This was another A4 which was fitted with AWS fairly late in life 8th to 19th November 1958 in the general scheme.

(opposite, bottom) You can still see the sheen beneath the dirt which has built up on SPARROW HAWK which is stood on the works reception lines at Doncaster shed on Sunday 7th July 1963 awaiting entry into 'The Plant' for scrapping. Condemned in June, the A4 was taken into works for the last time on Wednesday the 10th! *Courtesy Gavin Morrison.*

60019

Built: Doncaster, No.1866.

Put into traffic: 18th December 1937.

Original number: 4464.

Subsequent numbers:
    19 16th August 1946.
60019 14th October 1948.

Name: BITTERN.

Livery details:
Garter Blue with red and white lining: 18th December 1937 to 22nd September 1941.
Black unlined: 14th November 1941 to 21st January 1947.
Garter Blue with red and white lining: 7th March 1947 to 15th June 1950.
Dark Blue with black and white lining: 28th July 1950 to 8th January 1952.
Brunswick Green with orange and black lining: 12th February 1952 to preservation.

Side skirting removed: 14th November 1941.

Double chimney fitted: 6th September 1957.

Last major overhaul completed: 24th March 1965 Heavy Intermediate - Darlington.

Last shed: Aberdeen Ferryhill from 10th November 1963.

Condemned (Withdrawn): 5th September 1966.

Subsequent fate: Sold for preservation, 12th September 1966.

Comment: The only A4 allocated new to Heaton shed, it kept the same non-corridor tender (No.5638) throughout its life.

(above) With freshly laid track and ballast on the Down line, No.60019 BITTERN runs past Markham Moor with a Newcastle express in June 1960. Another Tyneside engine, the A4 had spent its first five year and four months working from Heaton but in March 1943 under an LNER (North Eastern Area) scheme implemented to cut down the number of different classes at any one shed, this engine was transferred to Gateshead where it was to stay for the next twenty years until a transfer in October 1963 sent it to St Margarets shed in Edinburgh. Within a fortnight of that event, BITTERN was off to the north again, to Aberdeen a life saving transfer if ever there was one.

(opposite, top) Settled in at its new home, No.60019 was a regular performer on the 3-hour expresses between Aberdeen and Glasgow, as here in June 1966. Working the morning train from the Granite City, the Pacific is climbing through the cutting north of Stonehaven. Note how the 'change of address' has transformed the external appearance of this particular A4.

(opposite, bottom) A nice portrait of BITTERN at Ferryhill shed in June 1966. Withdrawn on 5th September, it was purchased by C.L.Drury just one week later. Besides Doncaster giving the A4 life-long maintenance, the works at Cowlairs, Darlington, and Inverurie all gave some attention to No.60019 during its final two years in traffic. Note the Cowlairs trademark on the front of the casing the home shed name neatly applied in paint.

60020

Built: Doncaster, No.1867.

Put into traffic: 8th January 1938.

Original number: 4465.

Subsequent numbers:
20 15th September 1946.
60020 1st October 1948.

Name: GUILLEMOT.

Livery details:
Garter Blue with red and white lining: 8th January 1938 to 21st June 1943.
Black unlined: 7th August 1943 to 24th September 1946.
Garter Blue with red and white lining: 26th October 1946 to 18th March 1950.
Dark Blue with black and white lining: 28th April 1950 to 23rd October 1951.
Brunswick Green with orange and black lining: 30th November 1951 to breaking up.

Side skirting removed: 23rd October 1941.

Double chimney fitted: 7th November 1957.

Last major overhaul completed: 19th May 1961 General - Doncaster.

Last shed: Gateshead from 1st October 1945.

Condemned: 20th March 1964.

Subsequent fate: Entered Darlington Works for cutting up 29th April 1964.

Comment: *Another of the Tyneside based engines which was coupled to the same tender (No.5669 non-corridor) throughout but which nearly had its name changed to Dominion of Pakistan in 1947!*

(above) No.60020 GUILLEMOT approaches Grantham station from the south with a Newcastle stopping train in August 1961. This A4 spent virtually the whole of its life at....you've guessed it Gateshead! During its last 'General' a speed indicator was fitted and a repaint given but that was twelve weeks prior to this scene being recorded.

(opposite, top) This is the other side of No.60020 during that same month in 1961. Here, by the woods just south of Hatfield, the A4 is heading home with a rather smart 12-vehicle set of carriages. They must have liked the wartime black on Tyneside.

(opposite, centre) Like all of the Gateshead A4s, there was little requirement to have them coupled to corridor tenders and this tender was typical of the non-corridor type employed. Numbered 5669, it remained with GUILLEMOT throughout its life. This view was recorded at Doncaster shed on Monday 4th March 1963. Note the cleanliness! *Courtesy Gavin Morrison.*

(opposite, bottom) No.60020, in typical 52A garb, runs through Benningborough with the Up *HEART OF MIDLOTHIAN* on 6th August 1961. This was the only A4 cut up at Darlington works. *Courtesy Gavin Morrison.*

60006

Built: Doncaster, No.1868.

Put into traffic: 26th January 1938.

Original number: 4466.

Subsequent numbers:
605 26th January 1946.
    6 27th May 1946.
60006 2nd December 1948.

Names:
HERRING GULL until 1st December 1943.
SIR RALPH WEDGWOOD from 6th January 1944.

Livery details:
Garter Blue with red and white lining: 26th January 1938 to 1st January 1942.
Black unlined: 13th February 1942 to 22nd February 1947.
Garter Blue with red and white lining: 2nd April 1947 to 18th April 1950.
Dark Blue with black and white lining: 31st May 1950 to 5th September 1951.
Brunswick Green with orange and black lining: 17th October 1951 to breaking up.

Side skirting removed: 13th February 1942.

Double chimney fitted: 25th September 1957.

Last major overhaul completed: 10th October 1962 General - Doncaster.

Last shed: Aberdeen Ferryhill from 4th May 1964.

Condemned: 3rd September 1965.

Subsequent fate: Sold for scrap to Motherwell Machinery & Scrap Co., Wishaw, October 1965.

Comment: Re-named in 1944 in honour of the LNER's Chief General Manager. This was the second A4 to carry that name because the previous carrier, No.4469, had been written off on 20th June 1942 following severe blast damage inflicted during a German bombing raid on York in the early hours of Wednesday 29th April 1942.

(above) An undated broadside view of No.60006 SIR RALPH WEDGWOOD heading north at Retford with one of the non-corridor type tenders (this would be No.5675). The King's Cross based A4 was fitted with the speed indicator at a Doncaster 'General' in December 1960 and the 'newish' appearance of that equipment here may indicate the date of the illustration was not too long afterwards. Another of the A4s which survived the transfer to New England, No.60006 moved on to St Margarets on 20th October 1963 and then onwards to Aberdeen the following May where it managed to eke out work for a further fifteen months prior to being condemned.

(opposite, top) Having relieved an A1 from an Up express at Grantham, No.60006 heads for home in August 1961; looking as resplendent as King's Cross shed intended. Note that the A4 has the proper Gill sans figures on its front numberplate; many of the class did not get that modification.

(opposite, bottom) Ex-works outside Doncaster shed on 17th October 1962, No.60006 is ready to work home after a week of running-in.

60021

Built: Doncaster, No.1869.

Put into traffic: 19th February 1938.

Original number: 4467.

Subsequent numbers:
    21 25th May 1946.
    E21 5th February 1948.
60021 21st September 1948.

Name: WILD SWAN.

Livery details:
Garter Blue with red and white lining: 19th February 1938 to 21st February 1942.
Black unlined: 11th April 1942 to 21st March 1947.
Garter Blue with red and white lining: 30th April 1947 to 17th January 1950.
Dark Blue with black and white lining: 31st March 1950 to 4th July 1951.
Brunswick Green with orange and black lining: 8th August 1951 to breaking up.

Side skirting removed: 11th April 1942.

Double chimney fitted: 30th April 1958.

Last major overhaul completed: 17th November 1961 General - Doncaster.

Last shed: New England from 16th June 1963.

Condemned: 20th October 1963.

Subsequent fate: Entered Doncaster Works for cutting up 4th January 1964.

Comment: *One of the trio 60025 and 60029 were the others which were the last A4s to be cut up at Doncaster works.*

(above) Evidence of a Casual Light repair at Doncaster (16th July to 8th August 1962) can be seen at the front end of No.60021 WILD SWAN as it departs from Grantham with an express from Leeds to King's Cross in August 1962. This A4 was always shedded at depots located on the former Great Northern main line and had done two stints at Grantham - 1943/44 and 1948 to 1950 - prior to settling at King's Cross from 4th June 1950.

(opposite, top) No.60021 takes its turn with the Down late afternoon fitted freight from King's Cross goods yard known on the railway as the 'Scotch Goods'. The date is in June 1960 and the location is Gamston signal box. WILD SWAN was not long out of Doncaster after a Casual Light repair and it was to enter shops again in August for a Casual Heavy overhaul.

(opposite, bottom) Back on the expresses this scene was actually captured in May 1960 before that Doncaster CL repair and the northbound working of the 'Scotch Goods' No.60021 makes some smoke in the cutting near Gamston with an Up express.

60022

Built: Doncaster, No.1870.

Put into traffic: 3rd March 1938.

Original number: 4468.

Subsequent numbers:
    22 29th September 1946.
    E22 5th March 1948.
60022 16th September 1949.

Name: MALLARD.

Livery details:
Garter Blue with red and white lining: 3rd March 1938 to 2nd May 1942.
Black unlined: 13th June 1942 to 16th January 1948.
Garter Blue with red and white lining: 5th March 1948 to 18th July 1949.
Dark Blue with black and white lining: 16th September 1949 to 27th May 1952.
Brunswick Green with orange and black lining: 4th July 1952 to entering works for preservation.

Side skirting removed: 13th June 1942.

Double chimney fitted: 3rd March 1938.

Last major overhaul completed: 10th August 1961 General - Doncaster.

Last shed: King's Cross from 11th April 1948.

Condemned (Withdrawn): 25th April 1963.

Subsequent fate: Preserved in National Collection.

Comment: *Other than the fact that MALLARD was the first A4 to enter traffic with a Kylchap double blastpipe and chimney, there is not a lot more to say. Oh yes, it holds the world speed record for steam locomotives!*

(above) Only what you would expect from 'Top Shed', the world speed record holder No.60022 MALLARD looks in ex-works condition but is actually not ex-works at all. Under a stormy sky, the A4 pulls away from York with an Up express in October 1960. It was March 1948 before this A4 was coupled to a corridor tender; the one used in July 1938 was a non-corridor type, No.5642. BR therefore put this locomotive into the 'non-stop division' where it rightfully remained until withdrawn. What better advert for travelling by rail was there to have than the world speed record holder hauling a non-stop express between London and Edinburgh on a regular basis?

(opposite, top) This picture is a little bit of history in the fact that it reveals the return working of the last Down non-stop train known as *THE ELIZABETHAN* which MALLARD worked from King's Cross to Waverley on that final day, Friday 8th September 1961. The location of the illustration is Brookmans Park on Saturday 9th September and No.60022 has nearly completed it 392 miles run returning the stock and itself, as a SO service train, from the previous day's event. So, 800 miles in two days or actually about 14 hours of the 48, and most of those 800 miles were covered at high speed. Man and machine in perfect harmony.

(opposite, bottom) Another stormy sky, another high-speed run! MALLARD hauls an Up express in August 1961 and is climbing past Eaton Wood wearing its plaque which pronounced to the world its glorious achievement. Ex-works by about a week, the A4 has had a new AWS striker fitted and that is glowing red in the sunlight; the original ATC was fitted in February 1953.

(above) No.60002 SIR MURROUGH WILSON, in typical Gateshead external condition, climbs past Markham Moor summit with apparent ease in early March 1961 with a Newcastle-bound express. Remarkably this engine had only just completed its final General overhaul a few weeks prior to this scene being captured on film, so the Tyneside shed must have worked hard to get the locomotive looking like this already!

(opposite, top) The left hand side of MALLARD is presented to the camera whilst the Pacific is being 'turned' on the triangle at Grantham shed in April 1962. Magnificent!

(opposite, bottom) Suddenly standards have slipped. This undated illustration of MALLARD at Doncaster shed was possibly captured during the early months of 1963 when all things steam started to become superfluous to BR's ideals. Ironically the WD 2-8-0 alongside appears to be in a slightly better external condition than the A4 but look at that coal in the tender!

60002

Built: Doncaster, No.1872.

Put into traffic: 12th April 1938.

Original number: 4499.

Subsequent numbers:
     2 11th October 1946.
60002 14th May 1948.

Names:
POCHARD until 20th February 1939.
SIR MURROUGH WILSON from 8th April 1939.

Livery details:
Garter Blue with red and white lining: 12th April 1938 to 31st December 1941.
Black unlined: 7th February 1942 to 28th August 1946.
Garter Blue with red and white lining: 11th October 1946 to 19th December 1949.
Dark Blue with black and white lining: 2nd February 1950 to 11th July 1951.
Brunswick Green with orange and black lining: 14th August 1951 to cutting up.

Side skirting removed: 7th February 1942.

Double chimney fitted: 18th July 1957.

Last major overhaul completed: 26th January 1961 General - Doncaster.

Last shed: Gateshead from 10th October 1943.

Condemned: 4th May 1964.

Subsequent fate: Sold for scrap to G.Cohen, Cargo Fleet, July 1964.

Comment: *Apparently little used on either the pre-war streamlined workings or the post-war non-stops.*

(above) Another less than smart Gateshead engine, No.60001 SIR RONALD MATTHEWS leaves Retford behind and heads for London with an Up express in September 1960.

(opposite, top) Five months later, and with thirteen vehicles in tow, No.60002 is seen on another Down express but this time rounding the curve whilst descending Gamston bank on a glorious afternoon in August 1961. The AWS was fitted in March 1959 whilst the speed indicator was acquired during the previous January at that Doncaster overhaul. Note that electrification warning flashes have yet to be fixed.

(opposite, bottom) Condemned on 4th May 1964, this is how No.60002 spent some of the final months of its life leading up to that day. Residing inside the shed at Heaton on 4th February 1964, the Pacific had obviously done little work of late but whatever was ailing it was sorted out by the Heaton staff and it was sent back to Gateshead. Contemporary records show it working from 52A during the final days of April (and looking a lot worse than this). The illustration allows us to view the A4 with its mouth open and smokebox door ajar, a situation not often recorded on film. *Courtesy Gavin Morrison.*

60001

Built: Doncaster, No.1873.

Put into traffic: 26th April 1938.

Original number: 4500.

Subsequent numbers:
    1 16th November 1946.
60001 14th July 1948.

Names:
GARGANEY until 27th January 1939.
SIR RONALD MATTHEWS from 11th March 1939.

Livery details:
Garter Blue with red and white lining: 26th April 1938 to 27th October 1941.
Black unlined: 7th December 1941 to 2nd October 1946.
Garter Blue with red and white lining: 16th November 1946 to 28th December 1949.
Dark Blue with black and white lining: 10th February 1950 to 18th June 1951.
Brunswick Green with orange and black lining: 2nd August 1951 to cutting up.

Side skirting removed: 7th December 1941.

Double chimney fitted: 11th April 1958.

Last major overhaul completed: 5th October 1961 General - Doncaster.

Last shed: Gateshead from 26th April 1938.

Condemned: 12th October 1964.

Subsequent fate: Sold for scrap to Hughes, Bolckow, North Blyth, December 1964.

Comment: *Spending all of its life working from Gateshead shed, this engine too was apparently little used on either the pre-war streamlined workings or the post-war non-stops.*

No.60001 yes that really is SIR RON heading a Down express on Friday 14th July 1961, is approaching Drem where the branch from North Berwick joined the ECML, some eighteen miles east of Edinburgh. Gateshead's 'pride and joy' would enter Doncaster shops on the 31st of the month for its final overhaul and have a BTH speed indicator fitted; a repaint was also in the remit! *Courtesy Gavin Morrison.*

With the driver acknowledging the photographer, No.60001 passes Stoke signal box in August 1962 with a King's Cross-Newcastle express. Note that the engine is unusually clean for a 52A charge; perhaps 'Top Shed' gave it a quick going over before the A4's morning departure from London. Although all of the same maroon livery, the train comprises a nice mixed bag of carriage stock typical of this period of transition.

That's more like it! A filthy No.60001, again heading a Down express, crosses the River Idle at Retford in September 1959. Shortly after the completion of this particular seasons' summer timetable, the A4 went to Doncaster for its penultimate General overhaul.

No.60001 alongside V2 No.60967 at York shed on 20th October 1963. The A4 has suffered slight damage to the front of its casing and that dent remained with the engine until it was scrapped at Hughes, Bolckow's yard in Blyth during January 1965. *Courtesy Gavin Morrison.*

60032

Built: Doncaster, No.1874.

Put into traffic: 17th May 1938.

Original number: 4900.

Subsequent numbers:
    32 26th November 1946.
60032 10th June 1949.

Name: GANNET.

Livery details:
Garter Blue with red and white lining: 17th May 1938 to 22nd July 1942.
Black unlined: 4th September 1942 to 22nd March 1947.
Garter Blue with red and white lining: 3rd May 1947 to 3rd May 1949.
Dark Blue with black and white lining: 10th June 1949 to 16th September 1952.
Brunswick Green with orange and black lining: 24th October 1952 to cutting up.

Side skirting removed: 4th September 1942.

Double chimney fitted: 27th November 1958.

Last major overhaul completed: 22nd March 1962 General - Doncaster.

Last shed: New England from 16th June 1963.

Condemned: 20th October 1963.

Subsequent fate: Entered Doncaster Works for cutting up 6th December 1963.

Comment: *A member of the '20th October 1963 Club' which saw many former King's Cross A4s condemned at New England shed on the same day, No.60032's fate was sealed by the end of the year.*

(above) No.60032 GANNET nears Trent junction, Gainsborough, on a Sunday in October 1959 with a diverted King's Cross-Newcastle express. In the background a Peppercorn A1 works a diverted southbound express away from Lea Road.

(opposite, top) Back on the ECML in May 1962, GANNET leaves Retford behind whilst working a Leeds (Central)King's Cross express. During its lifetime the Pacific had been coupled to five different tenders and for the last five years had been attached to this one No.5331 which was to go with it to the scrap yard at Doncaster Works in December 1963. Whereas nearly all of the A4 class carried the words BRITISH RAILWAYS on their tenders shortly after Nationalisation, GANNET was one of the very few which did not. Note the continuously welded rail which had recently been laid on the Down side line.

(opposite, bottom) Going back in time slightly, we are in July 1960 near Eaton Wood as No.60032 hammers past with an express for King's Cross on a Sunday afternoon.

60005

Built: Doncaster, No.1875.

Put into traffic: 8th June 1938.

Original number: 4901.

Subsequent numbers:
5 3rd August 1946.
60005 9th July 1948.

Names:
CAPERCAILLIE until 14th July 1942.
CHARLES H.NEWTON from 19th August 1942.
SIR CHARLES NEWTON from 4th June 1943.

Livery details:
Garter Blue with red and white lining: 8th June 1938 to 14th July 1942.
Black unlined: 22nd August 1942 to 26th November 1947.
Garter Blue with red and white lining: 28th January 1948 to 10th October 1949.
Dark Blue with black and white lining: 23rd November 1949 to 6th October 1952.
Brunswick Green with orange and black lining: 11th November 1952 to cutting up.

Side skirting removed: 22nd August 1942.

Double chimney fitted: 8th June 1938.

Last major overhaul completed: 2nd November 1962 General - Doncaster.

Last shed: Aberdeen Ferryhill from 10th November 1963.

Condemned: 12th March 1964.

Subsequent fate: Sold for scrap to G.H.Campbell, Airdrie, June 1964.

Comment: The wartime exploits of the class have been documented many times but one particular working which is worth retelling about this A4 was the southbound working of a 21-vehicle train, crammed with passengers and weighing 730 tons. Typical wartime loadings perhaps but No.4901 managed to average 75 m.p.h. for some 25 miles north of York. Without the slow for the York stop, the distance may well have doubled that which was recorded!

(above) That is correct, it is a Gateshead engine. No.60005 SIR CHARLES NEWTON descends Gamston curve with a Down express for Newcastle in September 1960. The speed indicator was a fairly recent addition being fitted just seven weeks previously during a 'General' at Doncaster seven weeks, unbelievable or what!?. The AWS was another fitting which was 'new' in that it was put on during an earlier 'General' in December 1958; normal practice for Gateshead based engines.

(opposite, top) When No.60005 escaped to Scotland in October 1963, it was for but a short time because in March 1964 it was condemned at Ferryhill and soon sold on to a scrap merchant. Prior to that permanent transfer, the A4 was a regular visitor to Edinburgh on services from Newcastle and beyond. On a sunny evening in September 1961 the 52A Pacific was being turned at Haymarket shed and looked semi-decent but nothing was to last.

(opposite, bottom) Somewhere in England, which looks very much like Gamston curve, a clean SIR CHARLES NEWTON works south over the ECML with thirteen vehicles in tow on a date unknown.

60033

Built: Doncaster, No.1876.

Put into traffic: 28th June 1938.

Original number: 4902.

Subsequent numbers:
    33 31st October 1946.
60033 10th April 1948.

Name: SEAGULL.

Livery details:
Garter Blue with red and white lining: 28th June 1938 to 29th March 1942.
Black unlined: 27th May 1942 to 25th October 1947.
Garter Blue with red and white lining: 5th December 1947 to 3rd October 1949.
Dark Blue with black and white lining: 10th November 1950 to 7th May 1952.
Brunswick Green with orange and black lining: 13th June 1952 to cutting up.

Side skirting removed: 27th May 1942.

Double chimney fitted: 28th June 1938.

Last major overhaul completed: 8th June 1961 General - Doncaster.

Last shed: King's Cross from 21st March 1948.

Condemned: 29th December 1962.

Subsequent fate: Entered Doncaster Works for cutting up 23rd January 1963.

Comment: *A regular engine used by King's Cross on the post-war non-stops, it had been equipped with a corridor tender (No.5325) from 9th April 1948 at 'The Plant' works for such jobs.*

(above) August 1959 and No.60033 SEAGULL runs into York with the Down service of *THE ELIZABETHAN* a glorious day for the non-stop. The A4 had only just completed a 'General' and would have been in top class condition. Being coupled with a corridor tender, and under the charge of King's Cross shed, No.60033 was a regular on this train during the years when the non-stop ran. However, it is recorded that in the final season of 1961 this engine made just one return trip on this train. Other King's Cross engines which were regulars were Nos.60014, 60022, 60029, and 60030. Haymarket provided Nos.60009, 60024, and 60031. SEAGULL was one of the early King's Cross casualties and was condemned on 29th December 1962.

(opposite, top) The inauguration of the *ANGLO-SCOTTISH CAR CARRIER* on 30th May 1960 saw an eclectic bunch of vehicles brought together for the service which departed from Holloway at 7.50 a.m. arriving Newcastle at 12.30 p.m. (to drop off vans) and then on to Edinburgh (Waverley), arriving at 2.45 p.m. A balancing working left Edinburgh at 11.40 a.m., called at Newcastle (to pick up vans) from which it departed at 1.55 p.m., arriving Holloway at 6.30 p.m. Just days after the first Up and Down trains were started No.60033 SEAGULL of King's Cross shed was used for the Up service and is seen near Gamston signal box in the late afternoon. The road vehicles were inside the ten assorted bunch of vans behind the tender, with passenger carriages at the rear. Eventually, after the trains became quite popular, specially designed vans, with distinctive wells between bogies, were provided.

Later that month, No.60033 had charge of another Up express and is seen emerging from Peascliffe tunnel. This A4 and No.60034 were both involved in the 1948 locomotive exchanges (along with No.60022 which went to the Southern) and having to work on the London Midland Region from Euston station, the tenders of each No.5325 with 60033 and 5332 with 60034 were both altered at the rear end in order to facilitate the water cranes at Euston, and elsewhere on the LMR. The alteration required a small amount of the upper body being cut away. On their return to the Eastern Region, neither of the tenders were altered back to their original profile, and it is just possible in this illustration to see the cut-out on SEAGULL'S tender. Of course, by now the same two locomotives had exchanged tenders so that 60033 had 5332 and 60034 had 5325 (*see* section covering tenders). Whereas each of the A4s were scrapped, both of those tenders survived and it might be asked why Alan Pegler purchased certain of the 1928 built tenders Nos.5325 and 5332 when all ten were available at the time he purchased FLYING SCOTSMAN. Well now you know.

60034

Built: Doncaster, No.1877.

Put into traffic: 1st July 1938.

Original number: 4903.

Subsequent numbers:
  34 3rd November 1946.
60034 24th March 1948.

Names:
PEREGRINE until 21st March 1948.
LORD FARINGDON from 24th March 1948.

Livery details:
Garter Blue with red and white lining: 1st July 1938 to 8th August 1942.
Black unlined: 14th September 1942 to 15th October 1947.
Garter Blue with red and white lining: 10th December 1947 to 23rd October 1950.
Dark Blue with black and white lining: 4th December 1950 to 24th June 1952.
Brunswick Green with orange and black lining: 7th August 1952 to cutting up.

Side skirting removed: 14th September 1942.

Double chimney fitted: 1st July 1938.

Last major overhaul completed: 21st April 1965 Heavy Intermediate - Darlington.

Last shed: Aberdeen Ferryhill from 17th May 1964.

Condemned: 24th August 1966.

Subsequent fate: Sold for scrap to Hughes, Bolckow, North Blyth, October 1966.

Comment: *The final member of a class of locomotive which became legends in their own lifetimes, and most certainly afterwards.*

(above) Our final locomotive under review is No.60034 LORD FARINGDON which is seen heading north through Brookmans Park just north of London with a Down express in September 1961. This A4 was the only one ever to attend Stratford Works for repair actually only the tender, No.5325, required repair and that was carried out between 22nd and 27th June 1954. Does it count? Of course.

(opposite, top) Thoroughly at home! No.60034 tackled its new role in life with gusto and on a fine morning in September 1964 it is seen departing Perth with an express from Aberdeen to Glasgow. Altogether fourteen A4s worked from Aberdeen Ferryhill during those four years when the 'Streaks' worked the 3-hour trains; not altogether of course and some for only short periods before lack of main works attention and boiler changes caught up with them. During the period it had in Scotland, No.60034 was coupled to a non-corridor tender No.5640 but at withdrawal that tender was exchanged with the one attached to No.60024. LORD FARINGDON then went for scrap with corridor tender No.5329. One of the nice legacies of the A4 class at 61B was the fact that four of them were eventually preserved.

(opposite, bottom) With another Aberdeen-Glasgow express in tow, No.60034 is near Cove Bay with an afternoon service in June 1965.

No.60034 LORD FARINGDON and No.60016 SILVER KING at Grantham in August 1961. The latter is just drawing down to the train which the former has brought from London. The comparison in the cleaning standards between 34A and 52A are readily apparent.

(below) LORD FARINGDON performing a service of the last express passenger workings entrusted to the A4s the 3-hour express between Scotland's largest city and it's third largest. The date is sometime in September 1965 and the location is Allanwater, just north of Dunblane. The train is the evening Glasgow to Aberdeen express and the scene is wonderful. No.60034 was the last of the class to be put into traffic and nearly the last one operating for BR; that accolade went to Nos.60019 and 60024 which together worked two weeks longer than LORD FARINGDON. This final illustration in the survey is hopefully a fitting tribute to a class of steam locomotives which not only looked the part but could also perform as well as their designer intended.

A4 TENDER COUPLINGS - THE HISTORY (BR Numbers used throughout except where inappropriate)

TEN.   ENG.

1928 8-wheel Corridor Type: Tender Order 50A placed 30th January 1928 for seven tenders for Southern Area engines; Tender Order 50B placed 30th January 1928 for three tenders for Scottish Area engines. These Orders superseded T.O. 50 of 30th September 1927 for seven and three tenders to run with new 4-6-2 engines to carry Nos.60089, 60090, 60092, 60093, 60096, 60097, 60098, and 60091, 60094, 60095 respectively. The change to a specially designed 8-wheeled tender with side corridor was to permit crew changing on non-stop runs between London and Edinburgh and vice versa.

5323   60103 (5/4/28-23/4/29); 60107 (25/5/29-15/5/35); 60106 (13/6/35-23/10/36); **60023** (22/12/36-5/6/41); **60004** (23/7/41-3/2/48); **60022** (5/3/48-12/3/53); **60029** (12/3/53-20/10/63). *Cut up at Doncaster 31/1/64.*
5324   60107 (5/4/28-17/4/29); 60103 (8/6/29-19/10/36); **60026** (20/2/37-8/8/43); **60007** (8/8/43-1/2/66). *Sold.*
5325   60074 (10/4/28-2/7/28); 60065 (2/7/28-17/10/35); 60041 (17/10/35-7/12/36); **60009** (17/4/37-22/3/48); **60033** (9/4/48-28/5/54); **60034** (28/5/54-14/1/63); 60103 (15/1/63). *Preserved.*
5326   60081 (20/4/28-27/2/29); 60098 (20/4/29-30/6/29); 60092 (30/6/29-11/3/37); **60010** (17/4/37-6/12/37); **60011** (6/12/37-13/9/60); **60010** (15/10/60-29/5/65). *Preserved.*
5327   60048 (26/4/28-2/5/28); 60047 (2/5/28-6/5/28); 60048 (6/5/28-15/6/33); 60105 (10/7/33-24/8/34); 60096 (24/8/34-13/11/36); **60025** (23/1/37-3/9/45); **60028** (4/10/45-30/6/51); **60030** (30/6/51-29/12/62). *Cut up at Doncaster.*
5328   60070 (24/4/28-16/5/28); 60064 (16/5/28-17/6/30); 60099 (17/6/30-15/4/37); **60011** (25/6/37-6/12/37); **60010** (6/12/37-24/6/53); **60006** (24/6/53-14/7/53); **60010** (27/8/53-29/8/60); **60011** (28/10/60-11/5/64). *Cut up at Darlington.*
5329   60057 (26/5/28-7/6/28); 60053 (7/6/28-10/8/28); 60106 (10/8/28-4/9/34); 60105 (4/9/34-15/9/34); 60106 (15/9/34-25/4/35); 60107 (27/6/35-9/6/37); 60096 (30/6/37-6/9/37); **60007** (30/10/37-8/8/43); **60026** (8/8/43-29/9/52); **60032** (24/10/52-1/6/53); **60026** (1/6/53-20/1/54); **60003** (20/1/54-7/9/55); **60032** (7/9/55-9/2/57); **60024** (22/3/57-24/8/66); **60034** (24/8/66-3/12/66). *Sold for scrap with engine.*
5330   60089 (22/8/28-6/2/29); 60095 (6/2/29-20/3/29); 60066 (20/3/29-4/7/29); 60067 (4/7/29-10/7/30); 60064 (10/7/30-5/4/35); 60043 (5/4/35-9/2/37); **60028** (20/3/37-10/8/45); **60025** (20/9/45-24/5/55); **60014** (24/5-26/7/55); **60025** (26/7/55-21/7/58); **60022** (27/8/58-30/5/62); **60021** (30/5/62-20/10/63). *Cut up at Doncaster 31/1/64.*
5331   60090 (23/8/28-29/6/29); 60096 (29/6/29-24/6/32); 60090 (3/8/32-20/1/33); 60096 (20/1/33-18/7/33); 60090 (18/7/33-2/12/36); **60024** (26/12/36-18/2/57); **60032** (15/3/57-20/10/63). *Cut up at Doncaster 30/12/63.*
5332   60091 (8/9/28-30/6/30); 60100 (30/6/30-29/1/37); **60027** (13/3/37-29/1/48); **60034** (25/2/48-28/5/54); **60033** (28/5/54-29/12/62); **60009** (6/11/63-1/6/66). *Sold to A.F.Pegler 28/4/66 for £800.*

5000 Gallon Corridor Tender: Doncaster Tender Order No.54 placed 5th March 1929 for one to run with 4-6-4 engine No.10000 (60700) built by Darlington in co-operation with Yarrow & Co. Ltd.

5484   60700 (12/12/29-4/5/48); **60004** (25/5/48-17/7/66); **60009** (17/7/66-10/9/66). *Sold with 60009.*

5000 Gallon High-Sided Non-Corridor tender: Doncaster Tender Order No.63 placed 11th December 1933 was for five tenders to run with existing Class A2 (Raven) engine Nos.2400 to 2404, tender Nos.5580 to 5584.

5584   60043 (9/2/35-5/4/35); 60064 (5/4/35-17/9/45); **60003** (29/10/45-5/11/45); 60064 (19/11/45-4/9/61). *Cut up with engine at Doncaster.*

5000 Gallon Streamlined Corridor Tenders: Doncaster Tender Order No.64 placed 11th March 1935 was for four tenders to run with Class A4 engine Nos.60014 to 60017 (2509-2512). The front end was built up to match the cab profile to which it was joined by flexible sheeting for high speed trains.

5589   **60014** (7/9/35-28/1/36); **60015** (7/2/36-27/4/63). *Cut up with engine.*
5590   **60015** (26/9/35-21/1/36); **60014** (30/1/36-19/4/39); **60014** (9/6/39-23/8/45); Spare (23/8/45-7/11/45); **60014** (7/11/45-24/5/55); **60025** (24/5/55-23/7/55); **60014** (26/7/55-29/12/62). *Cut up with engine.*
5591   **60016** (5/11/35-29/4/48); **60009** (14/5/48-16/7/63). *Condemned 10/63 and cut up at Doncaster.*
5592   **60017** (18/12/35-25/5/39); **60014** (25/5/39-9/6/39); **60017** (9/6/39-20/10/63). *Condemned 30/12/63 and cut up at Doncaster.*

5000 Gallon Streamlined Non-Corridor Tenders: Doncaster Tender Order No.66 placed 6th February 1936 was for ten tenders to run with existing A1 and A3 engines to release their 1928-built Corridor tenders for modification to suit new A4 Class engine Nos.60023, 60024, 60025, 60026, 60027, 60028, 60009, 60010, 60011 (4482-4490) and 60007 (4498). Only six ever saw use with A4s.

5636   60073 (3/12/36-25/8/37); Spare (25/8/37-28/6/38); **60033** (28/6/38-30/3/48); **60009** (5/5/48-14/5/48); **60016** (11/6/48-19/3/65). *Sold for scrap, 5/65.*
5638   60098 (23/1/37-27/9/37); **60019** (18/12/37-5/9/66). *Sold with engine for preservation.*
5639   60042 (20/2/37-13/10/37); **60034** (1/7/38-22/4/39); **60022** (5/5/39-16/1/48); **60004** (4/2/48-24/5/48); 60700 (18/6/48-9/7/53); **60010** (9/7/53-20/7/53); 60700 (18/8/53-1/6/59). *Spare until sold for scrap 1964.*
5640   60100 (25/3/37-31/5/38); 60103 (2/7/38-15/1/63); **60034** (21/1/63-24/8/66); **60024** (24/8/66-5/9/66). *Sold for scrap with engine.*
5641   60043 (2/4/37-19/4/38); **60005** (14/5/38-12/3/64). *Sold for scrap with engine.*
5642   60092 (24/4/37-25/10/37); **60022** (3/3/38-14/3/39); **60014** (19/4/39-25/5/39); **60017** (25/5/39-9/6/39); **60034** (9/6/39-24/1/48); **60027** (11/3/48-26/7/48); **60030** (30/7/48-30/6/51); **60028** (30/6/51-24/6/52); **60003** (24/6/52-20/1/54); **60026** (20/1/54-21/12/65). *Sold for scrap with engine 2/66 but recovered and sent to Crewe Works for spares in No.60007's restoration. Re-sold 5/67 as a possible second water carrier for 60007 but later scrapped.*

5000 Gallon Streamlined Corridor Tenders: *Doncaster Tender Order No.67 placed 6th February 1936 was for seven tenders to run with new Class A4 engine Nos.60012, 60013, 60029, 60003, 60030, 60008, 60031 (4491-4497).*

5646   **60012** (15/5/37-20/8/64). *Sold for scrap with engine 3/65.*

5647   **60013** (12/6/37-27/12/50); **60006** (5/1/51-29/6/53); **60010** (29/6/53-9/7/53); **60006** (28/7/53-17/6/54); **60032** (17/6/54-12/4/55); **60013** (12/4/55-18/4/63). *Cut up at Doncaster.*

5648   **60029** (10/7/37-12/3/53); **60022** (12/3/53-21/7/58); **60025** (4/9/58-20/10/63). *Cut up at Doncaster 31/1/64.*

5649   **60003** (7/8/37-13/9/45); **60014** (20/10/45-6/11/45); **60003** (7/11/45-24/6/52); **60028** (24/6/52-29/12/62). *Cut up with engine at Doncaster.*

5650   **60030** (30/8/37-22/2/45); **60031** (24/3/45-29/10/65). *Sold for scrap with engine 29/1/66.*

5651   **60008** (4/9/37-1/4/57); **60021** (1/4/57-30/5/62); **60022** (30/5/62-25/4/63). *Cut up at Doncaster.*

5652   **60031** (2/10/37-14/2/45); **60030** (7/4/45-17/6/48); **60027** (26/7/48-3/9/65). *Sold for scrap with engine.*

5000 Gallon Streamlined Non-Corridor tenders: *Doncaster Tender Order No.67A was placed 4th November 1936 for three tenders to run with new Class A4 engine Nos.60004, 60018, 60019 (4462-4464) built to Engine Order 341A. Doncaster T.O. No.68 was placed 4th November 1936 for ten tenders to run with new Class A4 engine Nos.60020, 60006, 60021, 60022, 4469, 60002, 60001, 60032, 60005, 60033 (4465-4469, 4499, 4500, 4900-4902) built to E.O. 342. Doncaster T.O. No.69 was placed 4th November 1936 for one tender to run with new Class A4 engine No.60034 (4903) built to E.O. 343. Because five 5000 gallon high sided tenders Nos.5569, 5572, 5574, 5580, 5583 became available between June 1936 and August 1937 due to withdrawal of Class A2 Raven Pacifics, only nine new tenders were needed, and Doncaster plated these Nos.5667 to 5675.*

5667   **60004** (27/11/37-5/6/41); **60023** (25/7/41-30/10/64). *Sold for scrap with engine.*

5668   **60018** (27/11/37-19/6/63). *Tender cut up at Doncaster 12/7/63.*

5669   **60020** (25/12/37-20/3/64). *Cut up with engine.*

5670   **60006** (22/1/38-23/12/50); **60013** (8/1/51-12/4/55); **60032** (12/4/55-7/9/55); **60003** (7/9/55-29/12/62); **60022** (9/5/63 for preservation). *Tender renumbered to 5642 (the tender MALLARD was coupled to on its record breaking run in 1938) on 9/5/63.*

5671   **60021** (19/2/38-1/4/57); **60008** (1/4/57-20/7/63). *Went with engine to USA.*

5672   **4469** (30/3/38-6/6/42); *Tender badly damaged in the York bombing raid in 1942 when coupled to A4 No.4469. However, it was rebuilt and eventually re-used, coupled to Thompson A2/1 No.3696 from 22/12/45 to 12/12/60; it was renumbered 703 on 12/10/49.*

5673   **60002** (12/4/38-4/5/64). *Sold for scrap with engine 5/64.*

5674   **60001** (16/4/38-12/10/64). *Sold for scrap with engine 12/64.*

5675   **60032** (17/5/38-16/9/52); **60026** (1/10/52-1/6/53); **60032** (1/6/53-17/6/54); **60006** (17/6/54-3/9/65). *Sold for scrap with engine 10/65.*

No.60004 was coupled to this corridor tender No.5484 from 25th May 1948 to 17th July 1966 when it coupled to No.60009 and then sold with No.60009 for preservation. Originally built as a one-off for the high-pressure 4-6-4 W1 No.10000, later No.60700, the tender dated from 1929. Note the little circular window just above the electrification warning flash. The pair were seen at Perth in June 1964 whilst en route to Glasgow with an express from Aberdeen.

As early as June 1967 SIR NIGEL GRESLEY was running specials as No.4498 in Garter Blue livery and painted figures and lettering. Sold to the A4 Preservation Society in May 1966, they did not waste any time in returning the engine to its LNER pre-war splendour. Here, emerging from Cumbernauld tunnel, the A4 has a special working from Glasgow to Aberdeen.

Much of the source material of the information contained within this volume has come from Yeadon's Register of LNER Locomotives Vol.2.
Altogether, the Yeadon's Register amounts to fifty-seven volumes covering every LNER locomotive which existed, including the non-steam variety.
Details of the series can be obtained from the Publisher at: 0115 961 1066